Round House

for W.M.O.

Round House

Annette Macarthur-Onslow

. . . I who with the breeze
Had played, a green leaf on the blessed tree

Wordsworth. The Prelude 1805

Collins   St James's Place, London, 1975

William Collins Sons & Co Ltd
London · Glasgow · Sydney · Auckland
Toronto · Johannesburg

By the same author

MINNIE
UHU

First published 1975
© Annette Macarthur Onslow 1975
ISBN 0 00 216704 2
Set in Monophoto Bembo
Made and printed in Great Britain by
William Collins Sons & Co Ltd Glasgow

The observations and reflections
of a simple cottage life are
here preserved in notes and
diary jottings. Although, by
request, some details have
been altered, they remain a
faithful account of people,
plants and creatures, of
seasons and the countryside.

1962

At first there was a wall, a dry-stone wall, rising out of a bank and rearing into the sky. The road followed on a lower level curving upwards to a crest on which the clouds wandered like sheep.

Wind bent the grey grass, brushed humps of upland tumuli, and breathed into dewponds along the green ways where Nomads once wandered. Rock erupted in dun coloured outcrops and spilled from the sides of ancient quarries, while the land, fashioned by ice and sea, fell in curves and slides into unexpected dips and pans and rounded streamless 'bottoms'.

7

Then there were trees with gently swelling tips, and the
spaces between the trees full of horizontals, advancing and
receding. The tension lines of the hills were stretched like
guy-ropes pegged down out of sight, and the grey woods,
fields, walls, houses and outhouses were knitted all over
the landscape, scattering and collecting again.

It seemed that man and beast were integrated with every twig and thorn of this place; genius of time past, present and future infusing the new spring sap in each traditional hedge. Over all, the sun rose pale in one corner, and juggled the day-load of shapes and shadows, to set in a fiery, faggotty nest.

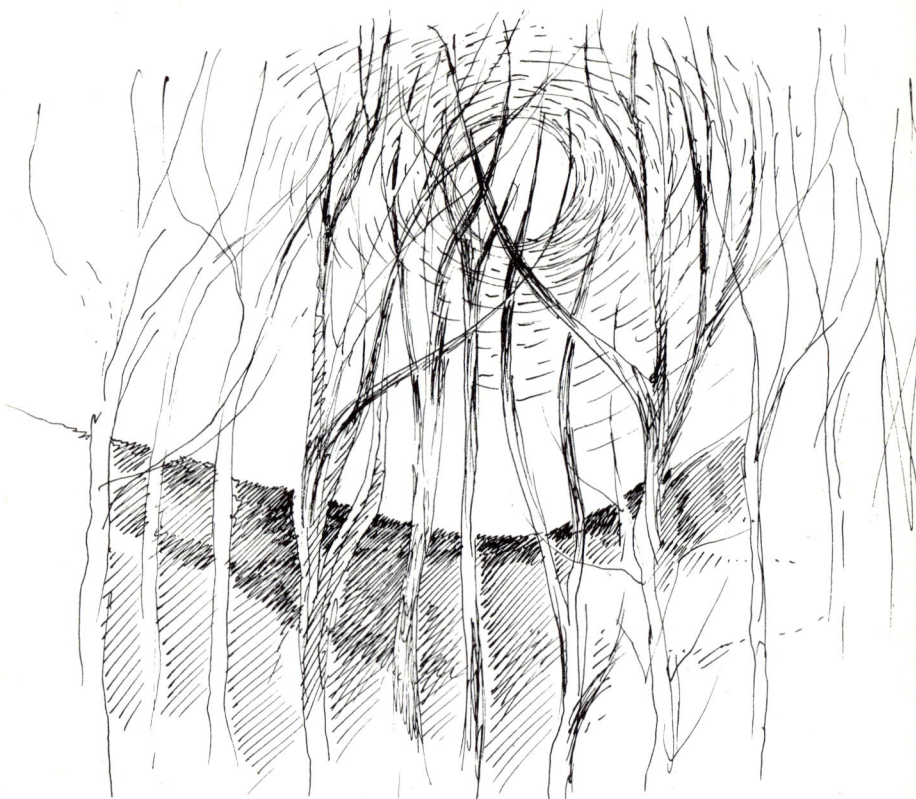

Winchcombe, Gloucestershire

I had been staying with the Haywards, Willi printing his poems on yellow card to flog in the local bookshop, and Sally, with newborn number three, being unusually

domestic. The cottage, Humblebee, in the lee of the wood,
looked down on the lesser landlord's Queen Anne
farmhouse and the greater landlord's castle. From time to
time, Willi, or whoever remembered, took a broom to the
Roman mosaic floor housed in a little hut across the kale
field. Romans had been big in this land. Even the pale
shelled snails were called Roman, though no one really
knew where they came from.

   At other times we walked to the top of the hill, to Belas
Knap, the Neolithic Long Barrow, and back, dragging a
load of sticks through the woods. Children ran down the
hill, across the fields to school and wound slowly
homewards, clutching the cream brimmed billy from the
dairy and fistfuls of sticky hedge flowers.

'For oo' Paul would say to his mother, proffering a bruised posy.

With each day, the city life, which I had fled, seemed further away, and I had an overwhelming desire to get back to the soil from which things grew; to witness first hand the mysteries of change and growth and depend on those basic things, wood from the trees and water from the ground.

In the hushed nights drawn by the Easter moon, nights softly and strangely guised, as we sat savouring poetry by firelight, I felt my desire rise like the smoke, swelling and curling in ever forming and unforming schemes, up the chimney and away to the moonlit presence of Great Humblebee Wood at the curtainless south window.

And as if guardian of some greater consciousness, the wood sent answer:

'Would you like a cottage of your own? We've found one . . .' It was my hosts, home from the pub, falling over their words with excitement . . . 'Of course there's no light or water and it's miles from anywhere, but it's got its own well, own woods and even its own valley . . . and it's got a studio which was used by a sculptor though it's been empty for some years now. They call it the Round House.

2

The drive to the Round House unfolded like a richly
patterned scroll. One moment we could see most of
Cheltenham, the Vale of Evesham and the Malverns, the
next moment we were hurtling half blind through tunnels
of bright leaves and flashes of pheasant-colour – down,
down, along a stream, across a ford, through a farmyard
and up a treacherous hill to a bleak field and a green-way,
the grassed remains of the old Chelt-Ciren road. Here we
left the car on the road, and were joined by two more
bodies. Ben an Irishman who knew the place, and Kath
Hayward who had lived at nearby Pinswell and who was
according to Ben an unrelated, 'lesser-crested' Hayward.
We crossed the field on foot through the gorse and
blackthorn.

   The wood, barely visible at first, rose steadily in two
curves like horns, two martial rows of black pines with a
gate in the cleft. It looked utterly forbidding with the gate
old and rusty and rarely used.

Inside the sentinel pines, were rows of beeches and copper beeches filtering pink and green light, new nettle nests and pheasant hens 'chock-chocking' to their chicks. The five of us led by Ben with his accordion, were suddenly inspired with the springiest spring, the brightness and colour, so that we skipped, almost ran, between the banks of bluebells to the cottage and the valley, while the Irish jigs that towed us along were backed by the domestic noises of every bird in the wood.

14

I had expected anything called Round House to be round like a mill or a garden folly, but this was a long house with rounded front and apse . . . a thoroughly pixilated house, roofed with stone tiles or slats, and built grotto-like of rough textured rag-stone, full of pockets and crevices harbouring shy toadflax.

The cottage had been empty for three years. Clifford, the last tenant, had died in Spain, and the house was full of his belongings – that is whatever hadn't been claimed by friends or rifled. Coats, hair-shirts and mouldy boots were rotting among the black shreds of paint, warped chairs and rusting iron. A neat, round hole had been shot through the upstairs window, and the chimney, victim of a gale, gaped down through another hole in the skylight to where its pot had joined the glass and plaster in a heap on the studio floor. Over the clearing dust, rubble and cobwebs, through the hole where the glass should be, there were gnarled and knotted apple boughs and the first new twisty leaves.

The air was electric with possibility.

Someone swept the quarry-tiled floor and tested the flue with a handful of smoking twigs. The fireplace, large enough to sit in, extended a massive chimney-piece like a Swedish oven, into the upstairs room and out of the gable through the praying fingers of rafters.

Someone else inspected the well at the bottom of the
hill – Pinswell.

Pyndeswell or Turpindeswell was the former name of
the Manor of Curburlye or Cubberley which was given to
the 'Nunnery of Gloster when Edytha was Abbess.'★

The sheep that roamed these pastures were driven back
to winter near Gloucester by a track that remains a still
traceable green way.

Ponies grazed in the field by the well. Slopes fell away
to other rich and thickly wooded valleys full of half
muffled cries and bellows and sounds of tree felling.

Somewhere a tractor was ploughing.

'You'll have to feed the cat . . .'

'Cat?'

'There's an old cat – been around here for donkey's years. Used to belong to Clifford. Got her own trapdoor into the house. She'll come and go – just put some food out for her. Her name's Minnie.'

All five filed down to Pinswell house looking for oddments of furniture.

Pinswell – the grey stone tiles glistening, and brimming water-butt shining under the inky yew. Young raspberries tangling with old canes, and squealing mice scrabbling all over the straw-filled stable. Suddenly strange eyes – yellow eyes with horizontal slits staring through the frame in the loose-box door. Bambi the goat, had somehow shut herself and two skewbald kids inside.

With thin dry udder the poor thing tottered dazed into the light and air.

An old striped scarf wound around Bambi's horns made a good puller while someone pushed. The kids frisked and gambolled and the strange procession, like a tired Bacchanal, filed slowly through the woods, the half mile to Connie's cottage.

Connie, who had once lived in the Round House, had now moved half a mile away to Hilcot Wood House, an older, stockier cottage, set half-way between the Pinswell group and the northern outpost of Needlehole (and Little Needlehole). None of these cottages had water or electricity and all relied for heating on wood from the timbered acres of which they were so much a part. Generations of wood-men, gamekeepers and shepherds had lived in these cottages scattered over the two miles of hill-top, until modern demands sent the land men back to the villages, leaving the poets, painters, potters and whomsoever to step into their discarded shells.

Legends had grown up about the 'Woods of Bohemia' and the wild ways of the artists – how wood 'nymphs' ran naked through the trees, and parties took trips on native fungi, or drowned in home-brewed rot-gut. But the loss of respectability (and a little agricultural iron-ware) was art's profit. The carousel with nature fermented an original vitality.

Against this back stop Connie wove her colourful way, coiling clay in the Round House shed, and cycling with a load of unfired pots, over the hills to Prinknash Abbey.

Connie's present cottage was a fascinating mess of plan and accident. The front door, which she had painted with two brushes to get the desired effect of olive and orange, glowed like the lichen spots on the roof. A Mexican lion with a head like a sun, roamed among the Bath stones.

Blue Persian ladies wafted through a ceramic glaze over empty milk bottles and oil lamps. Russian toy whistles, Dahomey bronzes, half finished clay heads wound in sacking, wire ligaments for sculpture gesticulating in corners, kittens rolling and tumbling on a spotted deer skin, all lightly bathed by the sun struggling through a dirty window pane.

Somewhere in the midst of the muddle was a sleeping baby in a basinet.

Connie generated a special spirit, It sang from the ever boiling kettle into the tea-pot. It curled fingers around steaming mugs and relished the hunks of wholemeal bread and cheese – and it purred.

In the window one graceful candle of white chestnut dripped petals from a Majolica jug. 'It's finished,' said Connie, and with an extravagant gesture, threw the spray to the goat. Bambi ate the flowers most delicately.

3

The decision to take the cottage meant weeks of scraping, painting, patching and plastering.

Ben came over to lend a hand; Ben who had lived in a caravan at Humblebee, given wild parties and slept in haystacks – Irish Ben, the 'scholar gypsy' with bony face and shaggy white mane, came in his own time and never when expected, unlike Frank the local builder.

Frank arrived on the stroke of nine to mend the skylight and upstairs window. Frank, a spare time poet, wrote satirical verse about the neighbourhood and obviously thought I was mad coming alone to a tiny cottage. He eyed the little truncated torso that someone had found and put in the garden.

'I can unnerstaand what men aartists draws but I be blowed if I can unnerstaand what 'oomen aartists draws.'

Willi too came to lend a hand, often walking the miles from Winchcombe, appearing from the woods, suddenly, silently, with gaze *distrait* and head full of lines.

Willi, unshackled from a publishing job, cleansing himself of London grime, was filling his eyes with the Cotswold hills.

He didn't approve of my painting the cottage:
"Should leave the walls as they are.'

Clifford had left some legacies, skylights and samples of home brewed plonk. Refusing to be spooked by any ghosts, I ceremoniously smashed and buried bottles and burned his clothes gone mouldy. It was bad enough sleeping on the floor upstairs, with the hurricane lamp on the chimney piece casting shadows on the rafters.

Past of shadows. Shadows to be cleared. Rambler roses, once tied, twine with honeysuckle. Toadflax tumbles from the rag-stone walls and buttercups besiege the yellow front door. Daffodils in the shadowy grass reflect the sun where it cannot shine, and primroses hide in cool places. The hands that hollowed the little amphitheatre and placed grey tablets along the bank, have carried every stone from the woods and the logs, unsawn, where they lay to season; have fashioned, in clay and plaster, the shapes now moulding in hessian and lovingly produced one perfect piece – an amber haired lady painted on ivory, placed in the sunlit window.

Meanwhile spring is fattening the landscape. Lanes are lush tunnels of hazy thickness, and succulent chestnuts cast inky shadows. Meadow grass, swelling with seed, ripples in the wind. The many coloured ponies of Pinswell field move in the landscape like the celestial horses of the Emperor of China.

Illusions about the lovely ponies shattered by a visit from the landlord. The riot act is read with reference to gates.

The ponies escaped through Pinswell garden and held night races in the barley field. Presume this has something to do with a sudden release of junior energy by the bio-chemist's family moving into Pinswell.

Paint a wall of the upstairs room (the yellow room) and pin up a print of LE MARECHAL DE FRANCE EN GRAND COSTUME.

The Yellow Room . . . lemon peeling over pink peeling over white . . . a gentle abstract wall drawing in the sun-soaked colours from wood and field, deflected from white rafters. The window, so carefully mended by Frank will not shut properly, and the landlord is peeved about the cost. Meanwhile in a half dream I go about nesting, filling the house with white furniture.

White furniture casting pale shadows on white walls – a chest of drawers in the chimney corner, white shelves breaking the wall surface; sombre blue of a fringed dhurrie; a bed, two high backed chairs, a bench for a table on which to spread a cloth by the fire, a basket for wood, a bottle for water, two black kettles and a pan.

This was the beginning.

Thursday was Cheltenham market day. I went in the elderly van with Connie, the baby bawling in the basinet, and Ben, in competition, squeezing Irish melancholia from his accordion.

This was not a beautiful market such as one finds in other towns built around some focal market place. This land was merely a vacant lot behind the railway yards, where sales people with makeshift stalls, seen in other towns on other days of the week, were busy outshouting each other against the cacophany of hens and dogs.

A section of junk and furniture was numbered in lots for auction. Tools, well greased and wrapped in bundles, farm implements, sofas, a Bedford van, and queenly among the rest, some cottage furniture – white, wooden and waiting . . . lot 45.

It comprised a wardrobe with panelled doors and brass hooks, a wooden chest of round-knobbed drawers, two pretty chairs with turned backs, a towel rack and a mirror.

I got lot 45, but not without a tussle. There was a little white haired man who seemed to outbid everyone. He was Charlie Fry, the junk king, who could buy cheaper and sell cheaper. He was piqued with me.

'Never bid against me, my dear!'

30

Then Connie winked at him and he grinned, After all he had landed the Bedford van for £35 and was loading it with quantities of things.

★   ★

Charlie, when one got to know him, was rather like an amiable ferret with his long nose, small wiry frame and white hair whisping from under his cloth cap. Connie he called Topsy and he whispered naughty stories.

His yard along the Tewkesbury road sprawled through an orchard near the gasworks, in a quarter of red brick cottages and 'none of your fancy stone'. Three or four acres straggled through a jungle of rhubarb and apple boughs against a back cloth of chain conveyors. Everything was organised in departments, chairs, beds, books and washstands, screens and masonry, antiques with the rubbish, incongruous objects vying with each other and to add to the strange atmosphere skewbald rabbits, when not prey to dogs or small boys, hopped and played in the rhubarb.

In front of Charlie's 'gingerbread house' was a small summer house covered with vines and filled to busting with old mattresses. 'Many a hot summer night I've spent in there kicking me sheets off,' Charlie would say.

When I bought some chairs, two shillings apiece – cheap because they had no bottoms though the frames were perfect, Connie whispered: 'Let's steal bottoms from other chairs.'

Then Charlie caught us and Connie said quickly: 'Oh, we're just pinching bottoms.'

'Eh – well I'll help you,' said Charlie.

Shelves were nailed to the kitchen wall. Book shelves made a good dresser. The wardrobe, too large to take upstairs was ingeniously dismantled by Ben and re-assembled up top.

Connie discovered some wash-stand tiles to fill the hole in the wall. They were not flat turquoise, but full of deep-blue depths and pale green surfaces. She also found a little brown coppery lamp.

Now there were treasures to
air – Provençal terracotta bowls
and a Freudian cooking pot
with a misfired pattern of
'petits pois', crocks, mugs and
tarot cards, toys, puppets, lamps
and an antique blue glass bottle
for two sprigs of spidery 'keks'.

The water-butt was cleaned
to catch new rain.

The well was cleaned where
it nestled among may trees.
Well water, cousin to
Cheltenham Spa, was said to be
full of minerals.

Spring never failed and water
never froze.

Oil lamps had to be filled and trimmed daily. There was a vestal dignity about the care of lamps. Each lighting ceremony was like a revelation with the gentle increase of the flame so as not to break the glass and the final snuffing to protect the mantle.

Was in the throes of lighting
a lamp when Minnie appeared
on the sill.

Memories of Minnie stealing
through the grass to feed and
creep into the night congealed
here into one trembling shape
mewing at the window.

This time she stayed when I
put my hand out – surveyed the
house, the furniture, the lamp,
and then, as though something
had suddenly clicked she
hopped down and sat by the
fire just as though she had never
been away.

4

The wood gods are powerful spirits in this place. How not
to offend them? Let the grass grow tall and rank and the
seed heads quiver.

Dock, thistle, blackthorn, bramble and briar all have
their place by this wood, and beside this house cottage rose
and peony with honeysuckle and willow herb.

The seven Chieftain trees are here, and the seven
Peasants.★ Who are we to decide what should or should
not grow?

Decision comes when I clear a weedy, smelling plot by the wall and find native roses, fox-gloves and lily of the valley all gasping for air.

Attack the nettles with a vengeance. A pale milky liquid, two ounces to a bucket of water, dispensed from a specially doctored kettle, the 'nettle kettle'. One drop, one leaf per plant is all that is needed to shake their mighty root systems. The hormone stimulates their growth to choking point. Within the hour the nettles droop, within five days they are black and shrivelled.

The water-butt is nearly dry.

Estimate I have carried sixty gallons from the well in one day. In the same day, dug three vegetable beds and had them christened the three graves by Kath, the 'Lesser Crested' Hayward.

38

Then, as if the Wood Gods approved, they sent a guardian with a pouch full of lettuce plants and a rabbit for the pot. Ernie Neal, the local keeper; gun at slant and golden dog Juno, 'I bin watchin' 'e while I were keeperin' roun' yere.'

I plant the lettuces in one of the 'graves' behind the house, where they look very pristine and vulnerable against the dark woods. Minnie promptly digs them up again.

Ernie's beat covers the woods on the West side of the Round House, from the Plantation to Lower Pinswell.

His detective eye roams over the trails and flattened patches of grass. He knows exactly what tussock harbours a partridge nest, or what animal has killed what other animal – where.

The balance of nature is almost entirely in the hands of the keeper. Everything orientated towards pheasants for the autumn shoot.

Most grain, fruit and shoot eating creatures are pests. Egg eaters and other predators are pests (poachers are in the latter category).

Foxes which provide good sport, are in the reserve class.

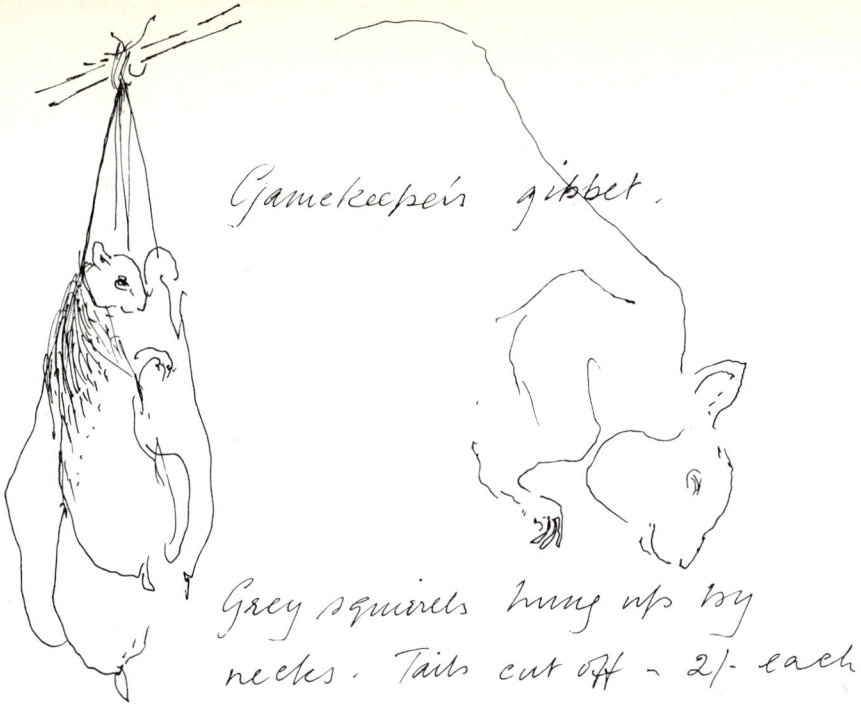

Gamekeeper's gibbet.

Grey squirrels hung up by necks. Tails cut off – 2/- each

The keeper's year starts in early spring, the planned chicks hatching under domestic hens in coops, the unplanned ones born wild.

All chicks learn eventually to stay around the feeding areas in the woods and come to the keeper's whistle for their ration of corn. To protect them the keeper surrounds the feeding areas with all sorts of paraphernalia; gibbets, clangers, and fox-scarers; rags soaked in creosote hung from trees.

By autumn when the crops are off the fields, a few remnant bales of straw are stacked for shooting cover on the edges of woods and swaths cut as feeding runs through the turnips.

Then sometime after the first of October, the woods resound with shouting and hissing and the army of beaters, led by the keeper, drive everything that can run, climb or fly out into the blast of guns.

Sport is a sideline of the woods, forestry their function;
but in between they are simply beautiful woods – woods of
many colours and textures, swelling and flowing with the
landscape; Fair Isle patterns of conifer and larch among
the broad-leaved trees, with hides and rides of
coin-spotted hazel and thickets of holly and yew. This is no
casual success, but the fruit of careful planning. The choice
of trees by searching tests of soil and temperature to suit
each patch of ground, and almost all the work of one man
– a squire, who nearly a century ago was a scientist
extraordinary; a dilettante botanist who combed the world
for exotics, planting arboreta of strange and new delights,
who as Fellow of the Royal Society, produced books and
papers on many subjects, noteably silviculture. His greatest
work, a co-operative effort in seven volumes, is still, after
nearly sixty years, a standard work for foresters.

So by chance, if not design, the thought and good
husbandry that created this visual poem of woods, created
also a harmony of landscape blending man-made with
natural thing into a vivid impromptu of that English art –
the management of Nature.

This is something to wonder about when one realises it
was not always so – that there was a time of awakening,
shaping and realizing the potential. There was a time when
most of the woods were merely patches of seedlings among
the wild acres and sheepwalks.

It is hard to believe that this country could cause Cobbett
to remark: 'Anything so ugly I have never seen before.'
and then go on to describe: 'The stone, which on the other
side of Cirencester, lay a good way underground, here lies
very near to the surface. The plough is continually
bringing it up, and thus, in general, come the means of
making the walls that serve as fences. Anything quite so

cheerless as this I do not recollect to have seen.'

According to Cobbett★ the name Cotswold Hills was tautological. *Wold* meant '*high lands of great extent*'.

According to Cox★ *Coteswold* came from the *sheepcotes* '*made there for the large flocks of sheep with fine fleeces there fed*' and *wold* or *would . . . a hill.*

Sheep, from early times, were the mainstay of the Cotswolds. Towns and villages fattened on wool. Exquisite market places, churches, manors and guildhalls were built, each in the style of the age, in the stone that stamps them Cotswold.

This oolitic limestone flaked by frost, stacks dry to form the pasture walls; new walls crisp as ochre fudge; stones streaked with iron and algae, gently becoming crusty grey, gathering orange lichens and shaggy astrakhan coating of saffron sericeum moss; stones slowly slipping off the centuries to collapse in feathery shale; the ghosts of old, old walls like bone pale vertebrae. Or rough set building stones, stones of barn and manor, rigidly faced with ashlar blocks and framed by chequered quoins. This is a world of stone, never far from the land's surface, pale unobtrusive stone, flecking the ploughed field or dancing in whims of masonry.

How easy by ancient rote to gather and shape this stone. How slender today the rule to build in the Cotswold tradition – even given the substitute blocks and pale coloured mock stone tiles aping the ancient slats. Nothing it seems can stem the flow of liver brick and purple slate creeping into the new estates. Barns are now shining metal and silos are painted steel. At least the tradition survives in the building of pasture walls. Dotted over the landscape in private therapy stonewallers labour with piles of stones –

the 'toppers' or 'combers' to stack like combs atop the wall; the 'jumpers' large binding stones to strengthen the wall; and somewhere astride the work, the 'profile' with its plumb-line.

There is something akin to a secret rite in the way a stonewaller works – quietly, by braille – almost like a musician fingering an instrument, listening for harmonies – gently relating stone to stone, shapes that are hard, creviced and pitted, until they lie almost as soundly as the very rock that shed them.

5

'What 'e need over yore way is a good dog to look arter
'e.' It is Shep the Westbury shepherd and we are sitting in
the Green Dragon. 'Got a good pup I can let 'e 'ave –
daresay she'd fetch roun' eight pound, but I'll let 'e 'ave er.'

I explain that I cannot have a dog because of the
pheasants.

'God bless you Shep, have a pint.'

Ben coined the title 'Green Dragoons' for this group
that gathers nightly clutching pints around the Dragon
fire. 'Shep' is a regular along with Charlie (good for a
song) and his fellow stonewaller Ossie Gittings whose
family hail from Shropshire. Foresters, gentry, ploughmen,
poets, from far afield they come to this little wayside pub
on the rise above Churn Brook.

For us from the hilltop the Dragon run, a downhill trot

through woods and fields, is simple gravitation (and a sturdy footslog home) but for others like Ossie, it's a long haul on a motor-bike – and so he arrives booted, helmeted and with mac pockets bulging with shell-fossils.

'Vind they vossils on west banks o' streams,' says he as he throws a handful of small stones imprinted with a tracery of shells onto the bar, 'an' this 'un 'e's a god! In old days thauy used to carry zich stwuns aroun' ver luck – there – e's your'n.' These are Ossie facts that he cannot explain further.

Charlie, Shep and the group in the corner are sitting glum, with clenched fists, 'spoofing' for the next round.

Behind the bar, ruddy-cheeked landlord 'Apple' Williams, nuggetty as his pub and sharp as an Orange Pippin, lines up the foaming pints, while his beaming coefficient Gladys collects the empties. Darts pop on the wall next door and conversation bubbles.

Tonight is a special Dragon night – night of the Midsummer Festival, when the witches will be purged from the woods by the firing and rolling of the 'Burney' wheel. There's a deer roasting on the bonfire and we are getting primed on 'scrumpy'.

But tonight we lack the staunchest 'Dragoons', the Johns from Needlehole. When they come down from London, for week-ends or holidays, it is as though the Genie of Soho or Fulham Road had suddenly popped the cork. Together with Connie they are a link with the past artistic junketings of the hilltop, and being mostly descended from, (or having opted into) the family of the redoubtable Augustus (the painter) they take to country life with an intuitive sense of place, relishing the good earth and the 'salt of it'.

As each of the five cottages on our hilltop has its own character, so do the people therein. Needlehole having been, as its name is supposed to imply, a point through which the stock (sheep and cattle) threaded from one place to another, somehow invites an extrovert life. It has the look of a coaching stage on the edge of Hilcot Wood.

So those 'birds of passage' the Johns, radiate into the countryside, spinning in a Landrover down Holly Drive to the Dragon, or making forays over the fields with their autumn coloured dogs.

Ben settles himself with the corner group.

'No music tonight?' – he rolls a fag and takes out a notebook. Tonight he's Ben the reporter: editor of *The Rooster*. Another night he might be Ben the leprechaun with his battered Irish squeeze-box – a kind of one-man cheer-squad or Puck for Master of Ceremonies.

Ben, once a classics scholar, has a sort of ragged grace, having thrown off conventional living and taken the role of 'gleeman'. His ways are the ways of a wild-wooder, by numerous footpaths and tracks. He can pace the woods at night with the stealthiness of a cat.

The most distant 'Dragoon' is Willi – wifeless tonight, he sits brooding, 'celebrating private visions' and lacing his 'scrumpy' with rum. Pleasantly dazed in euphoria he sees not, speaks to no one, catching threads of recognition that waft in the smoky air – weaving them into the fabric of his secret and personal myth.

Willi veils his excursions; this rangy, blue eyed Saxon, mixing Saxon understanding with Celtic mysticism. For him stone, tree and earthwork, man and all creation blend in one great timeless 'Dance'.

'Time gentlemen . . . and ladies . . .' says 'Apple' to start the feast . . . and in the cool damp air, on the slope smoothed for the 'burney' wheel – faces by firelight, rather squiffy – 'scrumpy' and rum, deer-flesh – songs, not very intelligible talk – witches cowering in the woods? Midnight; bright flash as the wheel (having soaked for days in oil and been fired) goes spitting and hissing over the grass; hurtling into the darkness to collapse in a shower of sparks. Stagger home on foot.

Trees by the gate moan. Light breeze, no torch, woods very dark and witchy. I clutch the stone 'god' in my pocket.

6

MINNIE HAUSGEIST – SPIRIT OF THE HOUSE – moving
with barely a sound except the flop of her trapdoor as she
leaves or enters. It is one thing to 'inherit' a loved place,
and another to take on its cat. While work is being done on
the cottage, while Ben, Frank and others come and go,
stripping walls and patching ceilings, Minnie is learning
once more to accept the presence of human beings. For
three years since Clifford died, she has been alone in this
cottage. When Connie took her to Hilcot to share with
the two Siamese, she simply glared at the cats, then sat
on the gatepost and pined. So back she was sent to the
Round House and fed by whoever left her food; catching
rabbits and mice.

A more cussedly independent, cautious or retiring cat;
a more domestic, well mannered or even comfortable cat
would be hard to find, except that her white fur never
stops moulting. 'Miniver, we used to call it' says Connie,
'threw it to the birds in spring.'

Most days she fends very well for herself, mousing all day and homing at night. But sometimes she reverses the process, sleeping all day and during the small hours shattering slumbers with strident miauls to present some bedraggled creature. 'Oh good cat, oh clever cat,' I have to say. A little praise, she is content, she purrs – sleeps. There is no hunger for these catches of the night (since she is well fed anyway). It is all showing off.

There is something infinitely harmonious about a cat asleep by the fire – a snail spiral of cat, a cosy muff of cat, a cat stretched along the thread of assurance but tempered as a well sprung spring to become in a moment electric cat, cat on guard, or cat in flight. Minnie was tuned to every footfall; registering every mood and quickly aware of any strange note, would slip away to hide.

'This had its practical use,' said Connie, 'she was our "early warning system" – part of the bathing ritual . . .'

Hip-baths were snatched in the Round House courtyard – on summer days. Minnie perched on the wall gave warning of any stranger's approach.

'What we did for baths then . . . we also used to run in the rain . . .'

. . . in preference to a hot tub by the fire or a visit to Cheltenham.

Cheltenham, famous for its waters, in its hey-day had three spas. It is now reduced to one, but remains of the old Montpellier Spa, apart from the stained glass windows ('Salubritas et Eruditio') is a row of tiled and panelled bathrooms, steaming with endless hot water, where bath-salts, towels and 'running' maids are part of the grand indulgence – where one can float the time away, gazing at Cheltenham's roofs through large Victorian windows.

(Spa waters, by the way, are not used for baths. These waters so rich in minerals, one *Takes* at the Town Hall Spa – dispensed from a splendid fountain-head into a paper cup.)

So much one takes for granted.

It is a sobering thought that folk in the past raised families in the cottages, washing in an old tin tub in the kitchen (the kitchen being the entire downstairs), boiling their water in the wash-house copper – water carried up from the well – not the lightfoot load of a single person, but labour for a family of five. Cooking was done on iron bars laid over the fire, the only perk being an oven at the side.

'Three children we had,' said Mrs Reynolds, 'the house was different then. The part that's now a window in the front – that was the door. The roof was thatched, but that was before our time.'

Keeper Reynolds started work at six shillings a week, soon after the turn of the century, when the old squire had two teams of oxen to plough the land, and bred all manner of rare and fancy sheep. 'Niver shore the sheep, just pulled the wool as soon as ever she started to moult.'

The children trotted the miles to the village school, and the parents walked to town on Saturdays.

'It seems we were always happy and always healthy,' said Mrs Stallard – 'Oh no, they were tough times,' responded Mrs Reynolds, 'we had our simple pleasures, but it's better now.'

These names, and others have a legendary ring. Families who spent their whole life long in the cottages. Stallard had had peopled the hilltop before the enclosures and been the district keepers for two hundred and forty years.

Now fragments of grand old families warm their hands by the village electric fires and peer at their television. The younger folk who no longer work the land are drifting away to the towns.

And Round House is changing shape once more –
becoming acceptably 'round' – symbolically round like the
hub of a wheel, centre for all excursions.

And at the core the hearth, burning logs by common
right; the smoke departing the chimney trailing the scent
of rabbit, herbs and butter, cooked on the open fire.

Whatever the state of the larder, whoever turns up at
meal times is somehow fed. This is the usual exchange
between the cottages.

In the long days of high
summer – days of breathless
heat, there are pub-crawls and
poetry.

The Haywards invade with
children on holidays, while
parents laze over charred steak
and rough wine and dream the
day away unheeding the sweaty
bunches of wildflowers and
raucous play. Willi engaged
with his summer angels – the
spirits that come with the heat
and disturb his peace of mind.

God Pan holds sway.

Softly the path to Needlehole
leads through forests of tall
angelica; through secrets of
Hilcot wood to where its
garden suddenly appears shorn
from the wilderness between
the cornfields, the Admiral Sir
Caspar John stalking tall
through the nettles with a
rotary mower. The cottage
leans on its buttressed wall and
in the space not yet a lawn,
there are half-naked bodies
baking in deckchairs: Rebecca,
Caroline and Phineas, heads
under newspapers, ground
strewn with (school?) books
and Mary in the kitchen
clucking: 'Why don't my
children do something!'

Studio is ready at last – skylight and walls patched, rafters oiled and rough stones coated with waterproof flat white. Move in with a blaze of colour jars, a trestle table and stool, a potato basket for rolls of paper and a rope handled sea-chest.

At the turn of the year, the folding time when the
stubble goes under the plough; when the old-time cottager
would have provisioned his larder for the winter – the
present populous of the hill are dispersed like leaves by the
wind, and most of the cottage doors are closed with
varying precautions.

Winter migration from Needlehole.

Official links to the Admiral mean a telephone which
sets Neeldehole a step above its neighbours. This, of course,
renders it vulnerable, so Caspar leaves a cautionary note:

> To all interlopers
> Trespassers
> Lay-abouts
> and others who trade on charitable human
> nature,
> This cottage is not yours.
> Nor is the firewood!
> In other words, give in order to
> receive . . .
> better still . . . stay away!

Some weeks later a reply is left on the table:

> To all Warlords, Sealords, Landlords – and others
> who trade on Servile Human Nature – The cottage
> belongs to Colonel B., the telephone to the G.P.O.,
> the firewood belongs to Mr E. – You belong to the
> Navy, the Navy belongs to us – so (Chorus) You
> belong to me, I belong to you. I can't give you
> anything but LOVE (Baby) . . . Goodbye, Goodbye,
> Goodbye.

As the telegraph boy whom I find one day, inspecting

my upstairs chest of drawers while on a delivery run explains: 'You never know who lives in these cottages.'

The usual posties, of which there are three, take it in turn to bring mail to the door, even if it means a half mile walk in wet or snowy weather. Wherever one lives in the British Isles it is the general rule that mail should be brought to the door.

This bothers one poor postman who is chased by steers in the top field. Apparently he thought they were bulls so has been leaving the mail with Connie.

Life is not often disrupted by animals – but to return to Minnie. I hadn't bargained on sharing the studio, the half way stage of her entrance into the house. Now there are muddy paw marks all over new drawings.

She has also found a friend – a three legged feral cat, ugly as sin, who caterwauls all night.

7

Smoke from stubble fires mingling with the mist. Smoke from other fires . . . the sacrifice of the ancient beeches along the top road. Chain-saws snarling and tearing at tree-flesh, heard all over the woods, and in the silences, the thundering crash of falling giants. Two lines of trees are ripped away leaving the remaining third line to claw the air in a helpless gesture. Day by day the dreadful procession has been advancing towards the Round House, the smoke from the funeral pyres rising skywards.

The saws bury themselves in the woods, half muffled, snoring and snuffling like a 'beast'. Sometimes the 'beast' hovers so close and roars so loud that I think my head will split. Then he trundles off into the depth again leaving a muddy trail, old cans and a smell of oil fumes. Fortunately the woods are not thinned so very often, once in five years is the year of the 'beast'.

Shooting . . .

New sounds . . .

The long drawn moan of a rutting stag across the valley. The hunt swelling, wavering and dying somewhere beyond the woods. Sometimes in brilliant close-up, but more often out of sight and out of phase.

Overwhelmed by the hunt one day. Hounds stream through the garden. Another day a 'ghost hunt' goes by on the other side of the Cathedral Wood. A blue frost lingers

on the north side of the wood. A white moon hangs over
the trees, straight and marshalled as trees in a Uccello
painting.

Snow! Autumn is at its peak and suddenly there is snow among the red cinders of leaves. Very cold.

This was a prelude.

The thaw that followed the early snow brought with it a grey damp for most of early December. The thickest smog for half a century settled over London and the Midlands. The smog followed the river valleys. It oozed around Birmingham and drifted along the Vale of Evesham to Cheltenham. There it was, half way along the shopping route, like a dirty tongue licking into the crevices of the hill. The Cotswolds remained above the murk in clear, cold sunshine. In the icy blue, the jets from Fairford and Little Rissington wove white trails like inverted skaters on a huge sky pond.

Ernie taught me to spot rabbit and hare trails in the frost dry grass and set snares of brass wire in the arc of a leap. Rabbits are creatures of habit . . . they establish their runs from burrow to feeding grounds and always jump in the same places.

'See them flat patches?' Ernie would say, 'that's where 'e jumps, so set the snare just this side of un.'

I watched with a kind of morbid interest; witnessed the loop poised almost invisibly on a split twig, the loose end staved and pegged down in the thick grass. I closed my eyes to the killing. Ernie could kill quickly and kindly . . . sometimes looking away from the work of his hands.

Snares I found quite immoral. There was a desparate time lag which must have meant agony for many little creatures. They were usually set early in the week. Then the haversack, emptied of wire, pegs and hammer, spent the rest of the week on its master's shoulder, trailing between the feeding grounds, collecting quarry.

One morning I awoke to a new strangeness – two handsome stags in the driveway. Two stags gently dappled as winter light, with vegetal antlers separating the rowan twigs; mealy faces and long necks stretched longer than the length of the body, seeking the clusters of red berries. Half interested they watched while I collected wood some twenty yards away. Only when I stopped to gaze did they melt like shadows into the forest.

At Christmas I went to London. Books were stowed, blankets folded and the cottage closed for the winter.

On Boxing Day it snowed and kept on snowing for three whole months. I was later told that the five barred gate at the top of the garden remained, for most of the winter, buried under a snowdrift.

1963

Returning to Gloucestershire after that long, tense frozen winter, when valleys had been besieged by snow and villages stranded, the air was still ringing with rescues, the earth still crackling with ice. There was ice on the road as soon as one left the highway, and snow below the hills meant winter still trapped in those valleys. At Round House, high and clear on its hill there were snowdrops, banks of snowdrops.

Though April already, spring was late from cold and little rain. The house was dry as a well sealed tomb; autumn leaves crackling and whispering; winter grass pale and flat; ground rucked and stitched with daffodil spikes, the tender sinews of cuckoo pint, ramsons and quilted primroses; sky brushed with pussy willow and the frivolous bunting of catkins.

Blankets and mattresses put to air, were draped on chairs like silent watchers. Hungry cattle in Pinswell field frolicked and bucked from trough to trough, trailing the hay and concentrates dispensed by Westbury Shep. Tractors purred on Monday's Hill. Top field was riddled with 'oont 'eaps' (mole hills). Mice, like moles, survived the snow, tunnelling under, finding grain, but rabbits and hares and sometimes foxes lay frozen to death, rotting corpses piled in the woodshed – strewn on the bank. 'Thirteen foxes was h'up by the resivoy,' said Ernie, 'all of 'em dead in the snow.'

Minnie had gone.

Minnie had been provided for – fed by Ernie. But when the old man was taken ill, she had set out alone across the woods, tracing Ben's footprints in the snow to arrive at Needlehole in darkness, cold, scruffy and so demoralised that after some warmth and food, she had quite forgotten herself and peed on his books through the upstairs floorboards. From that time she made HQ in the hayshed, hunting by day and homing at night.

Sunday 14th

All hell let loose, a beast of a day. Rain and gales. Trek to Needlehole tonight to rescue Minnie and to have supper with Caspar John. The womenfolk are away so Caspar and Phineas are batching – rough bread, a hunk of cheese and a ham boiled on the blue flame heater. Caspar mulls wine. Fire crackles against the storm. Then fed and battened down we listen to rain and fire. Attack the night again through sheets of rain and find Minnie cowering in the hayshed.

Cat-basket in one hand and torch and umbrella in the other, set out on the mile walk home with the terrified, crying cat.

Pause after walking through the boggy parts of the wood, and hear footsteps slurp-slurping behind. It is quite unnerving. The wood seems alive with eerie sounds. Pheasants and wood-pigeons whirr away into the night – their wings whistling and cracking twigs.

Minnie nearly escapes and in an effort to get her back in the basket, I drop both torch and umbrella.

Then a voice in the darkness breathes 'Hello . . .'

It is Ben with his white hair blown by the wind, going torchless home from the pub.

Monday 15th

Calm today, but a gentle gusting among the leaves, like puffs of steam from a safety valve, is a reminder that the 'wind machine' will blow again.

Green specks turn to leaves.

Beech tips, small, brown, furled parcels unwrap green paper 'kites'. An old pheasant cock has a roosting place on a stone near the door. Hens are nesting in the nettles – clutches of putty-coloured eggs.

Tuesday 16th

Sun – glorious sun. Plant mustard seeds, wild thyme and marjoram in the front bed. Carrots and spinach in the graves one and two on the other side of the house.

The wood is teeming with new springs after a day of ceaseless rain. Find one spring beyond the fir plantation. Suddenly the ground is open and water gushing into a dirty witchy pool, a dewpond in a thorn thicket. Water pours down the tree trunks (dark streaks on the soft green algae) or under old loose bark from where it emerges like sap at the roots – a frothy, bubbly ball. Around the pheasant feeders the keepers tap these watersheds by means of rough iron conduits into troughs. At last the beech leaves are flattened and the forest floor is a parquet of veins running hither and thither in variegated rusts.

Fronds of fern lie, sometimes still green, flattened like starfish by the snow, and from the centre the new embryo curls appear. Dog's Mercury, barely four leaves old, is very special now – each plant like a small star. Bluebell banks starting to show. There are deer tracks everywhere. Ernie sets traps for hares, but refuses to shoot deer! How strange the little winds that suddenly spring up out of the calm. It is as though the trees wanted to talk.

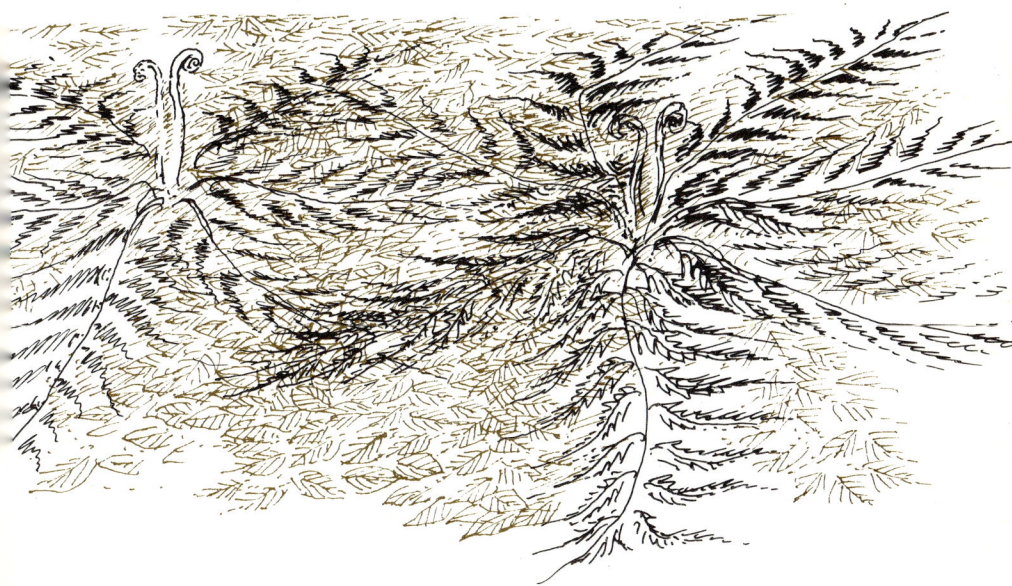

Thursday 18th

'You allus learn summut young 'ooman,' says Ernie.

Do the rounds with the old man this morning – the path through the top woods. Mercifully only two rabbits in all his snares. We pick turnip tops for greens. 'Cooked with a little vinegar – delicious,' he says.

I ask him what the yellow blossoms are on certain trees.

'Paume,' he says, 'what they picks to put in church on Paume Sundays.'

'Got rid of them thur badgers,' he proudly proclaims . . . Anomaly that the great lord pheasant should be preserved against the existence of this quiet animal.

This is the first day that I have felt spring really let
loose. This is the gentle weather when leaves can open
without fear. There is a fresh smell in the air. Single leaves
are identifiable on the end of twigs. Sycamore leaves
struggle open like wet fledglings to gradually spread in
flight. The ground is starred with new and exciting leaves
. . . shiny leaves, emerald next to olive; dark bottle green
ivy next to lettuce-green lords and ladies. Textures sharp,
pointed and flashy. Among the bluebells find a green
stranger – Herb Paris.

Shepherd brings ewes and lambs to Pinswell field. Clun
Forest sheep.

Cheltenham

Chestnuts out on the Promenade. Field day in Unwin's field. Mud everywhere.

Pinswell well is running high and the trough below bubbles like a crater. Clear some wood from the grove. Light lamps at 8.45.

Sunday 21st

More gales and rain.

Tuesday 23rd

A day worth waiting for. A brilliant day with the very smell of spring about it.

Westbury Shep says: 'This'll last a vew days, 'e can tell by the sheep.'

Sheep are contented in fair weather. Restlessness is a sign
of rain.

MAY

Tuesday 14th

Learning to master the weather moods of this place.
The elation of a sunny day and the depression of gloom.
One is more exposed and therefore more sensitive to these
changes. Like leaves against the wall, curling with cold,
bruised by the gale, only really opening and developing
in sunlight and calm.

JUNE

Saturday 1st

Summer. Temperature in the 70s. Fields.full of newly
shorn sheep. The black-faced Clun Foresters with much
agitation and circling dogs, file through the top gate from
Pinswell field, to the yards over the hill.

Flocks everywhere are gathered like dirty linen,
bleached and released. Temporary pens are thrown up in
the top field for a portable shearing unit. Ben 'try-any-
trade' enlists as a rouseabout.

Grass at least a foot taller. Peonies out and as beautiful
as I could imagine. Light glows through them and huge
bumble-bees vacuum-clean the yellow tufty centres. Can
see their actions in slow motion. They are so lazy in this
weather. Seeds have struggled along. Very dry. Herbs are
up. Snails hold night parties in the sage. A little mole has
dug its way into the flower bed by the wall. Seedlings
totter while I watch them.

In dry weather, moles move into the damper soil of
gardens.

Over this week-end cut the grass. Joined by three newly
shorn sheep who tip-toed through the woods from the top
field. Three rogues. They jump onto the low flat wall near
the 'three graves' and stand there for nearly a minute
choosing the juiciest vegetables before springing into the
garden. One wild swoop and I have pushed them through

the side gate into Pinswell field where they bully each
other to get at the pink salt lick. Then back through the
fence. (Only one third of the garden is walled). They stay
in the top part of the garden where they seem happy
enough with access to the salt through the fence. They are
like naughty children with a new found toy.

Friday 7th

Ernie arrives at 'sparrow's fart' to plant the rhubarb. He simply digs a hole and buries it.

Mends the gate and makes a clothes prop, complete with leaves. They stay green for a month or so. Mending the gate, he whangs away with axe, hammer and crow-bar while I hand him things like a surgeon's assistant.

Then he makes a saw-horse for the big logs . . . a few old fence posts and slabs of wood soaked in creosote against wood-worm.

The morning sun creeps under the tall grass; a rich yellow and lettuce colour. Dandelions have gone to seed and the garden is full of 'clocks' on long slender stalks. These 'clocks' are good rabbit detectors. When a dandelion clock starts waving frantically and slowly sinks into the grass, still upright, still waving, there is sure to be a rabbit on the other end of it having a good feed.

Take illustrating work into the garden today. Prop easel board against the largest stone seat by the wall. The stone is warm. The sun has baked it so that it remains warm when the sky clouds over. Earth and air are still and papers stay put while storms move around the sky – cu-nim clouds boiling and bubbling. Not a breath of wind. It is eerie.

Walk to the village to watch TV and back again, just missing the storm. The mist is settling and the woods are clothed in secretive darkness. Dandelion 'clocks' are perfect spheres, white and skeletal on their pale stalks caught in the mist light on the edge of woods.

Nearing Norbury Camp, I pass two huge stones, sarsen stones . . . haven't seen before. They look like grave-stones.

From this point the two valleys fall away, one over Lyde Bank, the other towards the Churn. Above the settling blue mists, over acres of woodlands, an orange full moon is rising . . . a giant dandelion 'clock'. The landscape is full of dandelion clocks.

Along the solitary line of beeches, against the darkened edge of the reservoir copse, there is a sudden scuffle and crash of breaking twigs. Nothing visible in the darkness, then four young deer appear on the brow of the hill, silhouetted in profile, two and two like Noah's Ark animals.

May hedges flowering and blowing in the lanes. Banks
of cow parsley. Festoons of white from hill to hill.
Dandelion down and moths in the grass. June breezes. May
flowers. Spring late, and oak and ash, the prophets of
summer, having tied in the annual race:

> *Oak before ash, in for a splash,*
> *Ash before oak, in for a soak . . .*

are flourishing together.

The water-butt is dry.

Tuesday 11th

Skylark sings at three a.m., long before the chorus.
Four fifteen the cuckoo calls. Walk to Norbury Camp just
before dawn, tracing my long shadow in the light of the
white, last quarter moon. Dawn breaks before I reach the
camp. Shadows melt into nothing and then reverse as the
sun comes up and I follow my long shadow home again.

Day colour rubs eyes and stretches new canvas. Sharp
lights glint and twinkle by the evergreens as spiders drift
on warming thermals.

In the glade the beeches are lettuce light – leaves nearest
the sky trapping lemon of the sun and filtering it through
degrees of lime and pink transparency, through a tracery of
vein and twig to dapple the very density of the air. At
the head of this glade, in a shock of green algae, a long
dead tree in half light of the clearing – preserved in its last
heroic pose – wrestling with snakes of ivy.

Thursday 20th

Pollen drifting. Sweet smell of haymaking. Fields raked
and combed by silvery, spidery whisks, then stranded like
corduroy, ribbed with piles of drying grass.

76

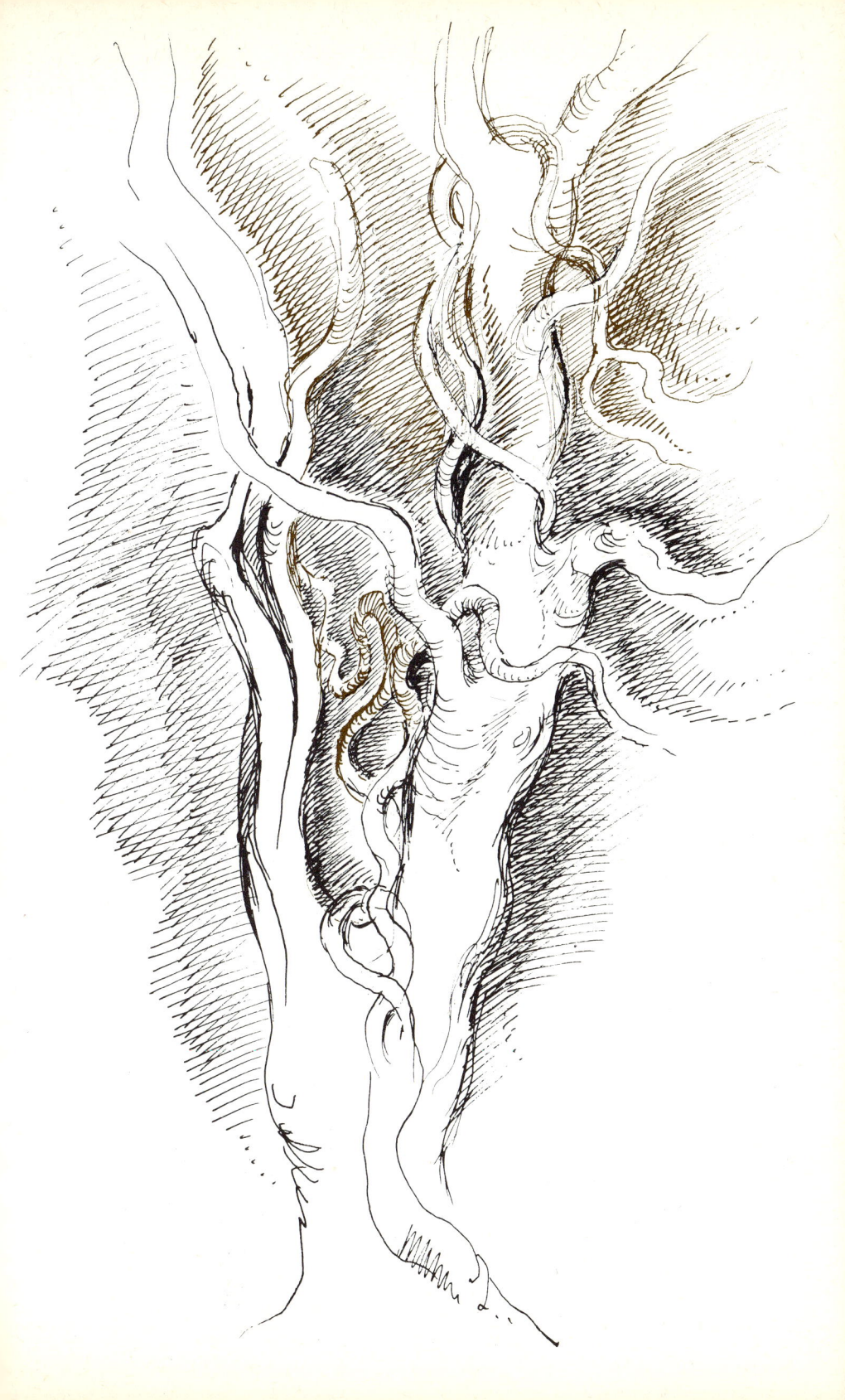

Friday 21st

Up at 5.30 . . . sticky and bed-bored, watching the cool
bees suck the yellow mullein stalks while Minnie, who
caught a field mouse in the night sits frowning where I
have thrown her (and the mouse) some hours earlier.

In the hot green stillness there
is a brooding spirit in this place,
an almost suffocating
expectation; not like the calm
before a storm, but like the
prelude to some indescribable
madness. It is almost dangerous
to let the imagination wander.
This is an unprecedented
intensity. In the stillness and
heat, this inner drumming of
blood vessels on the brain. They
are the silent cicadas of the mind
(remembering the dry
Australian summer) – drum,
drum, drum. (But that was a
summer of dust and
monotony). In this heat things
writhe and grow, being tugged
from the soil by the sun – tug,
tug, tug. Picture the intervals
like light waves, like the
'taches' de Van Gogh
frantically beating out a life
tattoo on his canvas. Yet it was
the Mistral which drove Van
Gogh mad – not the stillness.
Wind is disturbing, interfering.
The pattern of life is altered,
imposed upon. Maybe this is
what stirs most to action.

Grass has grown thigh high; been scythed; grown again knee-high; been scythed, and now at ankle height – Ernie will bring the dreadful lawnmower.

The lawnmower arrives. Neighbour from Pinswell passing the gate says: 'Number Two, The Pines.'

81

MIDSUMMER

Culmination of many days of heat – days when it has been
slow torture to work indoors while the world outside
purred and arched its back. Days when one's conscience
was pricked for not lazing and sun soaking – taking a
break in this sun-hungry country.

Woods – wells of shadow – light dappled on leaf screen
lapping the pool. Swim by the waterfall – hot, dusty,
sweaty from tramping. The icy shock of spring water.
Stand on stones; knees in ice; sun burning down through
the clear air as though focussed through glass.

Evening stillness. In stillness the spirits roam. Objects give out auras be they stone or bush; the rustle of a mouse can be heard through the grass – the glow-worm blooms on a dry stalk.

Plants in the still air are personalities. The mullein arches his rococco leaves and the nasturtium sits under his Chinese umbrella. Their inner dignity is unhampered by exterior forces.

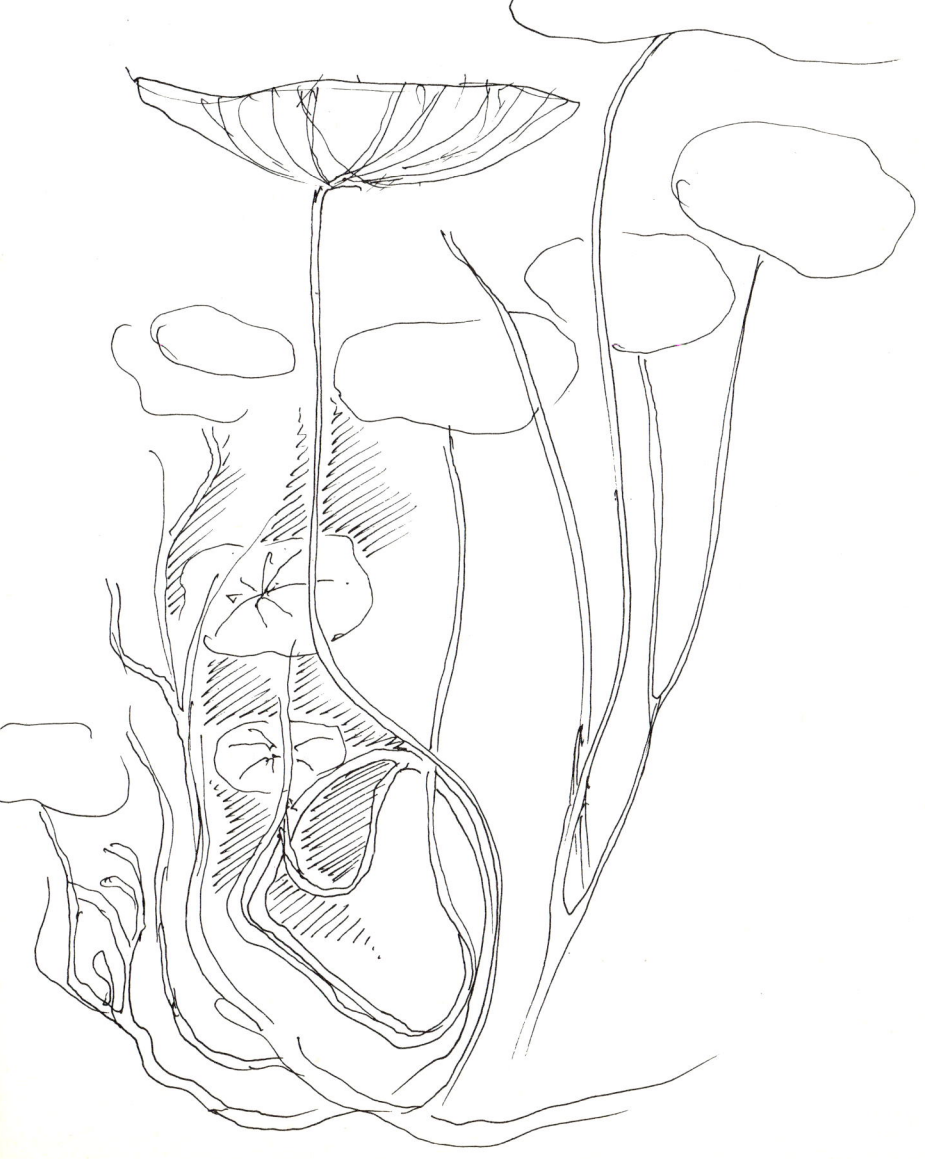

Grasses flowering – suspended in stillness. Umbellifers
flowering, white pats of cream or meringue in this season
of strawberries. They mount to heaven up hills, up trees;
elder flowers steeped in a bowl of gooseberries – adding a
flavour of ultimate mystery. But the grass flowers are
small and barely noticed unless one peers to see from the
bowed heads of brome, the dangling anthers – yellow
and brown men, minute symbols, lost in the microcosmic
jungle.

To either side of the gate there are houseleeks and
stonecrop. Houseleeks counter the evil spirits; stonecrop
means tranquillity. Here, as the red sun firms behind the
haze, ceding to the sickle moon, scribbled in twilight, that
ultimate pale when nothing sleeps, when flowers open and
seeds ripen; here, in the strange late linger, there is
suddenly a white dove. In this rare moment, when earth
tips over the rim of another year, natural forces seem all
powerful, and man no more than an anther strung from a
blade of grass.

JULY

Now chopped with the season's first mowing – the campions, stitchworts and speedwell. The year, sloped again towards winter sails on with remnant plumes – seeds pale, tasselled and fringed, corn hardening, cockle and poppy and the wayward limbs of charlock.

Flowers of high summer now fill the grass with their musical names: Clustered Bellflowers, Harebells and Meadow Cranesbill, Viper's Bugloss and Sheepsbit, Field Scabious, Broad Helleborine and Spotted Orchis, Birdsnest Orchid and Common Twayblade, Great and Lesser Knapweed, Pink and White Small Bindweed and Willowherb, and softly underfoot there is Silverweed which cures sore feet if worn in shoes, and Woodsage which, according to the dictionary, is still used medicinally in Gloucestershire. Ernie says he makes tea for the pheasants from Woodsage.

'Where do 'er learn gardnerin then?' says Ernie, watching me plant lettuces, crazy late in the season. It was a doubtful compliment and he gave the vernacular his own special twist.

There is a country economy of words to describe an action: going to town on business – businessing. Collecting wood – wooding, and as the shepherd who told me that the had been 'sheepin' all mornin'' when asked what he had been doing to the sheep said: 'I were feetin' un.'

Sunday 4th

Ernie arrives in his finery, breeches, leggings and tie with a foxy pin, tweed hat and blue jay's feather, golden labrador Juno and hazel walking stick.

Ernie's sticks are a speciality. He cuts them from green hazel which grows tall and straight. He takes a measure from elbow height to ground. Then he trims the stick clean leaving a forked end which he pares down to fit the crook of the thumb and forefinger.

Hazel hardens with age, and the older the stick the stronger.

Of course he never carries a gun on Sunday. This is his off duty gear. 'Been arter that thur carrion crow all week, an' there 'e were today large as loife – knew I din 'ave me gun.'

The old man loves being photographed, particularly in his Sunday best. He poses this way and that until, with the morning slipping away he suddenly says: 'Well, I'm off now – 'ave 'e done camer'in?'

SEPTEMBER

The world has drawn grey shower curtains under a ceiling
of lead. The veiled harvest moon barely sees the ragged,
greying crops, while gale-blown rain sweeps sheet on
sheet from the Atlantic, eastwards against the path of the
sun. Springs burst, high streams become cataracts and
valley rivers – torrents. Boots smack into treacle pudding
mud.

Bath has been flooded.

Day after day the rain gusts, calms and gusts again,
leaving the woods dripping even in moments of calm.
Grey fur sprouts on leather, wood and wool; green 'fur' on
bark and stone; moss flowers and grows incredibly lush
and tall; exotic toadstools, unseen at other times, loom in
the depths of the woods, and plaster casts in corners of the
garden, grow coverings of fine green hairlike grass.

Ernie says that the weather 'played hammock' with his
roses.

89

Wednesday 18th

Somewhere out there where the weather comes from, the American Long Range Forecasters, who predicted the wet, have forecast thirty days dry, and miraculously the rain has ceased as though someone had turned off the tap.

Now the warming sun curls tongues into cracks of stone, and reflections from glass and water shine through the cool shadows. A bias of faint gold displaces the morbid grey in the tattered remnants of corn. The landscape starts to whirr and purr and bees to buzz and wasps, seeking the sticky, sweet jam suck juice from the plums, leaving the round skin bags still hanging from the trees.

On Monday's Hill the combines move in stately file at ship's pace across the horizon. Ben suggests that Caspar John, in Admiral's uniform would look very fine atop one of these machines.

Friday 20th

Walk over to Monday's Hill to watch the harvesting. The third and last cut has just been opened – about twenty acres on the steepest slope of the hill. An old red machine mows around the edge of the field, while two new yellow machines cut across the standing corn. (Corn in this case is barley which they are heading for the brewery).

The yellows go at their job with a speed and precision which is marvellous to watch. They gauge the exact width of the cut, wheeling and turning one behind the other, up and down the slope leaving a trail of straw but never an inch of standing corn. As the cutting area decreases and the wheeling and turning increase, they look like polo ponies in very slow motion with rather mulish heads, the augers, stuck out at gawky angles.

Every so often they pause to disgorge the barley grain through these augers, into waiting trucks which are towed to a central dump. The air is full of dust. Wheels bump over the myriad stones. The late sun glints on the shiny metal. Eventually the hillside is razed to low mounds of straw in long regular stripes. The great machines stop twisting and turning, and lumber away over the hill.

93

Saturday 21st

Autumnal Equinox – the turning point of the year. Today on Monday's Hill there are ritual scars, as mysterious as ancient runes.

Winchcombe. Homecoming of Willi after recuperation in Merlin's Cave from 'writer's cramp' and an overdose of family.

> *No self to hide in a kind litter of leaves,*
> *In a daze of trees, in a soft walk of hills.*

Sunday 22nd

Today they are setting fire to the stubble and burning the straw. Mist mingles with smoke from the dross fires drifting around a windless sky. The sun looks more like the moon.

Men with torches of oil-soaked rags firing the straw; grey ghosts through the smoke trailing bright orange-yellow flames which lick along the mounds.

The shepherd has moved the sheep from Pinswell field. The gates are open and riders come and go. A pounding of hooves, and suddenly a mock hunt bursts into the field. Trails have been laid in ultramarine powder – (takes weeks to wash off). Someone has put a GONE TO EARTH sign on the old dog kennels at the bottom of the hill. The immaculate pony clubbers mill around waiting for the next scent, making little sallies back and forth across the valley.

95

There is an introvert strangeness about mist . . . the half
appearance of things. The mown fields have variegated
stripes where machines have brushed the stubble now this
way now that.

From north west hill, migrating swallows everywhere;
wires vanishing into nothing; houses vague and suspended
in air; owls screech in the daytime. Hedgehogs. One two
nights ago on Minnie's plate. Several on the roads, more
of them dead than alive. In the garden at night they seem
to tread so heavily on the fallen leaves that at first I think
it is deer.

Monday 23rd

Apples reddening.
Tiny windfalls bumps in the
grass. Quicksilver squirrels
coursing the beech boughs.
Half the apples bitten into. Am
bottling the salvage with the
last of the rhubarb. Morning
dew; mist and spider's webs
turning gold with the day, then
heavy mists that remain all day,
barely cleared by the sun.

OCTOBER

Colour is creeping into the woods.

The willowherb is bright red on the edges, through oranges into greens in the thickets. Bryony, yellow in places and purply-brown in others, hangs necklets of red and green. Thinning elders are a pale bruised colour as though stained by their own berry juice. Brambles, heavy with fruit have here one yellow leaf, there one russet. Find a wierd deathly place . . . thistles blown, standing like ragged sentinels. Hogweed skeletons, gaunt tufty spears on the skyline.

Tuesday 1st

Sale at Cockleford. Walk over this evening. (This is the best time of the year for walking when crops are off the fields.) Everything has sold except two chicken 'arks'.

Evening light. Frosty mist in the valleys. All the machinery, red and yellow looks very festive. The lower hills softly curving and covered with light green pile. Sheep and lambs in pens. The Clun Forest sheep that once lived in Pinswell field.

Rough pens thrown together. Hurdles made from ash strippings. Several sheep trucks waiting. There are little holes along the side – peepholes for the sheep? A white, shaggy dog is leaning from the cabin window of a brown timbered truck. Tractors and pick-ups are moving off. Machines unlicenced for the road will go on trailers.

Ben thinks he might buy one of the arks as a home for the ROOSTER.

Thursday 3rd

Ploughing, harrowing, drilling, rolling – the land is scored with ever widening brown gashes. Seagulls flying inland ahead of equinoxial gales hover like flung spray in the wake of the churning soil, while rooks, those 'old men of the land', stroll 'hands in pockets' behind the plough, picking up small worms and molluscs – rising lazily to skim the stubble as the ploughman begins the next cut.

Machines they do not fear, but approach on foot and each flock, black and white, shrieking and cawing, is 'pulled away' by invisible strings – whisked like magician's capes, they rise, circle, and take off – gulls to the far hills and rooks to the trees.

The gulls are now beyond recall, but the rooks will keep hovering, never settling for more than a moment while watched.

'There I were up ahind the tractor,' said Ernie, 'tryin' to get a shot at them thur rooks to scare 'em off since I couldn' get near 'em on foot. Do 'e think one of thauy beggers 'ud come down ahind the plough? Not while I were up there.'

NOVEMBER

Gales, rain, blackened leaves and mud – and now fog, and through the fog a new sight on the hills – drilling rigs.

Drills are being sunk for oil in a charted line across England, and our hilltop is one of the victims of this plan. Huge vehicles churn mud in the gateways and overalled men with American accents and tin helmets move between the rigs like nightmare characters in some strange film. Car trouble with the mist and damp. Twice towed by jeeps, now the car has broken down at Seven Springs – kindly at least by an AA post. The place is just shutting down for the night, so the men, off duty now, cannot help, though they obligingly open the roller-blind a crack to reach for the telephone and contact the garage. I am then left sitting in the fog.

Bitter cold.

Peer into the fog, not seeing the road, only moving headlights emerging out of the gloom and disappearing again. They move like Will-o'-the-wisps, crossing and re-crossing the twisty cross-roads . . . a pale lightening in the fog and then, from fifty yards or so, the two points become lamps. This is no fairyland, this is Limbo, nothingness and gloom. Not a passing cheery word, just the swish, swish of tyres on the road and unidentifiable shapes hurrying out of sight, out of mind.

The garage men collect the car, and I walk home two miles. The fog clears on the hill top. There is starlight. Pass the sinister oil rigs and hurry on home.

Back at the Round House the world clicks the right way up again. The moon is rising through trees at the top of the garden, and two soft winged owls drift from branch to branch.

The rooks are over Norbury Camp again – over this
ancient and lonely place among the clawing branches of
half-bare trees. An endless practise of 'circuits and bumps'
– forming, breaking, stacking and landing always on the
same tree – squabbling and jostling, circling and touching
down again.

From westward away to the Severn estuary, where
heavy clouds hang veils of rain, a flock of gulls, rising and
dipping in the gusty wind, are flying straight up the valley.

They fly directly to this hill as though drawn by a
magnet – straight into the restricted area of the rooks. No
rules of the plough following etiquette here – the two
clash in a battling, wheeling mass of black and white. I
hurry on to the village to beat the approaching storm.

Roof is mended. Cracks cemented, road chipped and pot-holes filled with stones. Rain has washed down the gravel. Writing this after a hard day.

Pithy old beech smells like peat on the fire. Minnie nestles like thistledown in the window, never disturbing the seed-heads poised delicately as spider's webs.

DECEMBER

Full moon. Frost – at first barely perceptible . . . a silvery glitter in moonlight on dry leaves, and with the lowering of the mercury, a stiffening of grass underfoot; ice cracking into slivers and spines on puddles. Then, by the end of the first week, accumulated crystals forming rime to the thickness of each twig on each bare tree.

Sheep in single files making green tracks in the white, and wood casting blue shadows to the north. The Round House is now in a frosty hollow – the sun barely touching its roof as it rolls over the horizon like a big lazy orange, and disappears again. The white-coated roof has distinct patches to either side of the chimney where the warmth has melted the frost. The yellow room is closed off to form a vacuum and keep the house warm.

Minnie sleeps by the fire, curled in her snug box like a possum. She wakes, eats and sleeps again and ventures rarely into the frosty air

Mice have come into the house from hedge and field. All night long they scuttle, rattle and squeak in the wall partition. I trap, on average, three a night, mostly in the cupboard under the stairs, and Minnie, whose expectations have led her to believe that the cupboard holds a never ending flow of dead mice, sits and 'burns holes' in the door every morning.

The iron hard ground is easy to drive on. The Post Office van still comes to the door, but riding is impossible, hunting is off, and the usual daily clatter of hooves on the drive is replaced by soft footfalls, as grooms and sometimes owners lead their mounts, hunched and steaming under heavy rugs. Ewes with swollen bellies stand breast deep among the turnip tops, pawing at broken turnip flesh with tapered hooves. Shreds of wool strung on briars, sway in the north wind.

Below the frost line (which at this stage is about the tops of hills) new fresh colours; browns, greys and yellow-greys, brilliant greens and reds. Fields are now visible between the trees in normally impenetrable thickets. Some ploughed fields show changes in soil colour. Leaves trapped around the mossy-green trunks are russet all over the floors of woods. Streams, hidden at other times, suddenly admit to curves, waterfalls and small lakes.

Dashes on foot to the village. Path by the beeches,
Norbury Camp and Bulbarrow Wood across the Park
between the copses, down the stony path to the footbridge
over the Churn, up again through the tall trees to the

cottage backs and the school yard, the stone roofs and the gardens, bare but for a few red rows of rosy pickling cabbage.

The store is always full of people passing the time of day with responsive Mrs Tucker. My wild-wooder appearance, boots, wind-cheater and pack usually gets some comments: 'I wouldn't live up in those hills,' says Margaret behind the counter, 'not with all those snakes.'

Play acting the simple life was all very well. It was when one had no choice that it lost its charm – so reckoned those who had moved from the woods to the village, and could hardly be expected to understand the rewards of independence or rarified air, the silence and light that was special to these hills.

Being a free-lance also had drawbacks, but at least it was blessed with time. Even time spent wooding or trimming lamps seemed more rewarding than flicking a switch and paying the ultimate bill, and the days of most fulfilment were the days of special light when one could just stand and marvel.

Winter days when the eye-level sun across the valley turned the trees long shadows to phantom besoms, sweeping great arcs; days when the light raised hedgerow and copse on shadowy stilts and crept into the serpentine worlds of leafless branches, or searched with fingers tapering into the forest behind the cottage; bewitching light, where, one day gathering brash for kindling between the long brown columns, I was startled by the sudden rush and thump of a large animal, and a hound, golden as the sun itself went bounding along the track to Norbury Camp, followed in due course by two bowed personages deep in talk. For a moment the vignette between me and the sun was full of strange happenings, seemingly more important than they really were, because of the golden light in which these spirits moved.

On the same track in late evening, two silvery does leaped the garden wall and vanished into the mist. Then I heard screams . . . eerie, human-type screams in the valley . . . so spine chilling that I stood rivetted waiting for the next horror. But instead a dog-fox yapped and the screams answered. It was a vixen.

On the 18th snow was expected. The ground froze and the air turned blue with that slight pinkness in the clouds that heralds snow. But the morning of the 19th was pale and clear with a heavy frost making beautiful feathers in heaps on the ground and rococo fern patterns on the kitchen window panes.

Sixteen degrees of frost were recorded in the village.

There must have been at least twenty degrees here.
Connie's water tank froze and burst and Connie came back
from Buckingham with new baby Julius, to face hanging
nappies around the 'Fyreside' heater, and cleaning the well
while two year old Collette ran barefoot in the frost.

Troubles aside, Christmas came on with all the ritual
ingredients. With most of the trees bare, the cottage
background was reduced to firs, pines and glossy black ivy.
The only berry-bearing holley-tree for miles around, hung
festive red clusters over the driveway – where for two
hours a day it was caught by the sun.

Tow-haired children from farm cottages brought great
baskets and climbed the tree. Posties drove to the door
when they could, or ran, blowing on whitened fingers,
across the fields. Actually the post office was so constipated
that mail was days, sometimes weeks late, but no matter
. . . I thawed out the frozen posties with coffee, and
sometimes Ernie too on his pheasant feeding rounds.

One day as the strains of a
squeeze-box came lurching
down the track, I looked up
from the drawing-board to see
Ben, the leprechaun, in his holey
flannel jacket, come to deliver
his Christmas ROOSTER.

Christmas shopping in Cheltenham and Gloucester was much like shopping anywhere else when one climbed down from the hills and walked among the steaming crowds. There were moments however, such as the day that I took crippled little Mrs Neal to Gloucester, and when our bags were full, we walked in the white silence of the College Green, beside the Close, where Cathedral choirs were practising.

1964

Snow came.

Sky took on Earth's dark values and over a strangely lit horizon, seemed to reflect it. Then with the rising wind came the advance guard of flakes, small parties of 'scouts' searching hither and thither, circling wind-tossed before falling – damp, absorbed by the warmer ground. Then, as the wind grew sharper, starting to adhere to blade and twig. Later came the 'troops', more definitely blown, keen as needles pelting the landscape, the thin white stipple becoming a blanket. Behind them, legion upon legion were shaken like feathers from a pillow, out of the sky across the valley. Several inches fell. Then the wind dropped. Earth lay silenced and bound.

Tree trunks were striped evenly down one side by the plastering force of the wind. Coppice and branch, made suddenly wonderful, blossomed white lace. Puffs of breeze sent flurries of powder, and as the sun warmed and melted the rime, small drops fell, pocking the ground with neat round holes. As the day wore on the snow was inscribed with scribbles, the hieroglyphics of unseen creatures, and over these traces were blocked in daubs of colour, scoured in ice on the bleached canvas – the trees, so vivid by day, at night became darkly armed, brooding, bristling over the moon's pale mantle, brushed with glitter.

This was our day of snow. The next was slush. The rest of the season was more like spring with bursting buds and primroses flowering. Then spring was like winter, arriving frigid – a clenched hand that fears to open, letting sharp blasts through the cracks in the fingers. At length some warmth convinced the blossom and amid white specks came the peony buds, the first cuckoo, and shep playing mid-wife to lambing ewes. And there was Ben on his 'lady-bike' peddling ROOSTERS at sixpence a pop, mapping the lanes of ROOSTERSHIRE.

Impermeable, all weather Ben, nimble as Mercury, hoary as frost, who had traced his way in last Year's snow along the tops of remembered walls, this winter had had 'office' troubles. But three forced moves in as few months, with all his 'estate' in fertilizer bags – plus ostracism from local shoots and being 'bugged by the light in the East' – far from lowering the morale, found him now together with one, Jim Partridge, fellow accordion artist; like a creature in a mediaeval masque, he was perched in a high and windy place, playing squeeze-box duets to the moon.

'The Light in the East' of Ben's former view, had been the light of a lonely farmhouse – home of the new Messiah. One could hardly blame the Messiah – she was a small girl, not yet two. Nor could one blame her mother, a television writer, so it must have been the spirit father, his own rumbustious countryman, the roving ghost of GBS that finally routed Ben. The ROOSTER's creator couldn't compete with the higher literary work being typed from the master's spirit dictation. He had had enough trouble of late with his basic bread and butter.

The general excuse for Ben's being barred from beating

at local shoots was that Ernie suspected him of pinching
pheasant eggs and 'boiling them in a kettle'. They never
were the best of friends. The first time I heard Ernie
mention Ben was in connection with a shoot. 'There 'e
was the . . . . . . on the job and reading a book!'

It was too much for Ernie who had been brought up to
toe the line and pull the forelock. His formative years were
spent in livery, and middle employment in charge of a
team of green-clad under-keepers around whom he ran
rings in a smartly turned out pony trap. Ernie was a
perfectionist and the latent policeman in him would never
tolerate the 'poacher class', particularly intellectuals. One
simply had to mention the democratic 'Green Dragon' and
he would hiss: 'That Place!' Ernie had a blind spot for the
Dragon and Dragon types. He had no taste for the

bonhommie dispensed by jolly 'Apple' Williams, whose
wit still sparkled on 'dry rations' (Apple's term for
prohibition) nor did he warm to the antics of his own
nephew Charlie.

Nightly after the yarns and clink of coins spoofing for
the next shout, the hiss of the mulling iron drawn from the
log fire, the pop of darts and maybe a song or two . . .
when 'Apple' had doused the lights for the umpteenth
time, the doors were shut and the yard cleared of the
clutter of transports . . . some would repair to Charlie's
Cold Slad Rabbitry for a final touch up of rhubarb wine.

There were always the few who finished up on foot, like
Ben that spring night in Hilcot wood . . . torchless and
stumbling through the trees. On such an excursion some
years before, my Round House predecessor, Clifford, had

padded home through Pinswell wood, bang into a mantrap trip-wire, with loaded gun fired skywards.

It was Ernie who apologised that time, and paid off with a new 'joke' in the form of a dead fox which he set up to look lifelike in the Round House kitchen. Clifford had wanted a fox pelt, but this was more than was expected.

Had Ernie thought more kindly of Ben he might have gained more space in the ROOSTER, not that Ben was short of matter with characters like Sid Hunt, the Council roadman who could mimic a cuckoo or gad-fly or Bobby Belcher the Lyde Wizard, who sold cure-all pills of rabbit's dung and flour and carried a half-length stick which he waved like a wand, spiriting away warts and headaches and terrifying thieves into confession. Or the nameless cottager who won himself a flush loo by embarrassing the squire's family with his bucket ritual . . . 'and they on their way to church and all' . . . or Shep Newman of Rapsgate whose legendary feats at sheep shows gave rise to improving tales swapped over the bar.

'Took 'is sheep to Smithfeeuld show by passenger train,' they said, 'had zum trouble gettin' 'em through the unnerground an' hup the hescalator. Thauy Lunnoners wazn't much help.'

In fact the remarkable shepherd had cadged a lift to the city and being stranded some two miles from Earl's Court, had paid a fellow a pound to guide him with his two sheep through the bombed sites and derelict lanes to the show where he carried off a first, second and third prize.

'You should hev seed thauy 'oomen fly inside thur 'ousen 'an shut the doors when they seed them sheep acomin' down the street.'

The local opinion of London and Londoners did not amount to much, and feats of the countryman in town were usually borne home like banners of triumph. Townsmen were considered an inferior race who had lost their sense of touch with natural things; had forfeited a heritage of green space for brick and mortar. As Ernie said: 'The trouble with Lunnon is 'e can't see it fur 'ouses.'

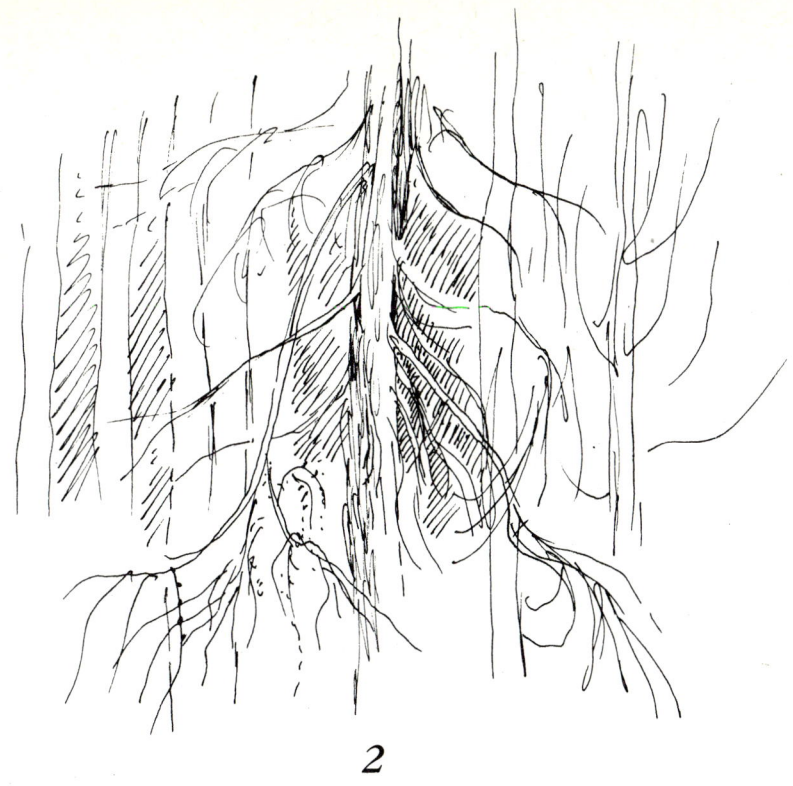

2

The woods, like the people around them, varied in character. Hilcot being a wild and airy wood, a wood full of flowers and scrubby hazel, differed from Mercombe wood which was planted, and which, because of the large number of conifers was a closed and dark wood, a wood concentrated within itself and affording little to no view of the outside world. A phrenological chart might have organized the areas of this wood into fields of logic, levity and poetry with here and there the obedience of the various planned rides converging on a central route which coursed the downward slope in a graceful curve, brushing on the way memories of stone walls, extravagant splashes of bluebells and soaring flights of willowy ash.

At the base of the slope was a grove of Thuya – quiet grey-green evergreen, like marestails in some twilight pond all steeped in pink brown light. Here, where the paths met and melted into some indistinguishable beyond, would, I thought, have been fitting place for a temple.

By day when the sounds of Mercombe Wood merged
with a thousand landscape sounds, there was little to
distinguish the sounds of the wood unless it were the
mysterious scuttlings, ruslings and sudden sallies of hooves
through the undergrowth. But at night, when the farm
and village sounds were hushed and sheep and cattle
drowsed, browsed or slumbered in the fields, the woods
became magically alive and the very trees seemed to wait
breathlessly as the night prowlers began their fearful work.

One sensed the dreadful employment even on a
relatively silent night, but then there were times when the
league of predators shouted its intention to the winds.

Dog fox yapped to screaming vixen and a dozen or more pheasant cocks exploded in a shattering cacophany. Owl called to owl, and echoing owls in neighbouring woods threw the cry away and away. All night long while the hunter's tally-ho rode back and forth, those rival agents, stoat, weasel and feral cat moved silently under cover on their endless dark missions: their secret killing.

One could enter the mystery of the woods only if one moved softly, sat quietly – one could enter those other worlds, small worlds with special laws. If one waited at the cottage window and did not rush to investigate the happening outside – did not break the spell.

Often at first light I surprised deer in the garden, or stood transfixed by the well while fighting bucks clashed antlers not twenty yards away; often saw, as close, a stoat check, poised upright on its tail, and then flip, suddenly fired like a small torpedo ruffling the Dog's Mercury, Above the leaves, from time to time and further and further away, the frantic shoe-button eyes peered back. At such times I could have wished myself protean – passport-holder to who knows what forbidden regions.

Deep in the valley by Hilcot Brook, where woodlands met in sombre groves of cyprus and redwood, where box and yew crouched darkly on steep banks; coots nested under shining laurels and a lone white swan cruised like a battleship 'midst a fleet of corvette ducks. Here, in the dreamy waterscape of ponds, was Lyde Cottage, the most woodland, woodland cottage.

Among the sterner farm cottages, both Lyde and Round
House, inclining to cottage orné, wore a frivolous air.
But whereas Round House could claim some link with the
land, Lyde was quite 'other worldly'. Here life was paced
by the water's flow; the down, wind-sped, among the
kingcups; the lazy drift of fish.

Dwellers of the cottage, creatures of other worldly
pursuits like scattering crumbs upon the water or watching
long-tailed tits snap the air, while gazing out one morning
saw a rabbit dancing on the lawn 'enjoying the bright
morning' they thought – until suddenly, in a frenzied leap
it fell on its side and in a flash was ripped by the tiny
creature, only then visible, clinging to its neck. It was a
weasel enjoying its blood breakfast.

★   ★

I first came across the badger's setts in Mercombe wood
by following a trail, a wide-enough-to-be-human,
well-beaten trail, obviously not human because of the low
boughs it passed under and the thickets it passed through.

The setts were in the south east corner of the wood, in
a clean floored beech grove, wedged between tracts of
bramble and hazel thicket and opening onto a field. There
were two or three setts with well swept doorways which
pronounced the badgers At Home, a sprinkling of
fox-holes and at least one identifiable badgers' playground.

Will to survive has driven the badger into a secret world.
Seldom is one seen in daylight. Most hunted and most
tenacious, saved by its strength and digging powers, it
cleaves to the earth by day and moves under cover of
night.

The badger is fastidious. The first of its waking minutes
at dusk are usually spent removing old bedding and
clearing the entrance before making off to the fields. It is
a scavenger rather than a hunter, feeding on insects,
especially wasp grubs; domestic scraps if it can get them,
carrion, frogs that may hop in the way or rabbits which it
takes from snares, though unlike the greedy plundering
fox that will kill for pleasure and feed at random, it will
neatly finish a meal of rabbit and turn the skin inside out.
The legend of the lamb-eating badger is apparently
unfounded. Even its threat to eggs is barely proved. It
always dines out; never brings food home, but instead
trundles dry grass or leaves to make up its new bed.

127

Tuesday 19th

Set out at 9 p.m. (just after sunset). Old clothes, anorak
with hood, anti-midge cream smeared around wrists
and hair-line, sketch-pad, flashlight with red cellophane
filter, box of matches and ground sheet. Follow eastern
ride by tall pines. A young deer startled, but curious, keeps
parallel on a neighbouring bank some fifty yards away,
alternatively watching and bounding through hazel
clumps, all four feet together.

On the edge of the badger wood, light match and watch
smoke. Breeze slightly south east and barely discernible.
Take up position down-wind of sett – a large sett with
many holes. (Studied the geography of this in daylight).
Have a good view of three holes, the rest hidden by a bank.
Trail of leaves to each entrance shows that all are in use.
About 9.25. Horizon still light. Rustlings on bank about
fifty yards away. It is deer; three does gambolling like
lambs up and down the bank in perfect silhouette; tails in
air. A fox slinks by quite close, unnoticed by the deer.
Silence . . . all disappear.

Little catspaws of breeze explore outer edges of the
wood. Roosting pheasants disturbed, cackle and clatter
into the night. Silence. A scratching sound and a thump
(quite heavy) thump, thump, thump over the leaves. It is
a squirrel. Six feet away it sits up – flick, flick, flick and
with one more flick of its question-mark tail, it is off.

Twilight is giving way to moonlight when the first
badger appears – a body grey as the dusk itself and head
streaked like the moonlit patches. It is visible only by the

movement of its nose – a keen nose raking the air for
scent – catching an invisible bellrope on which it
hangs and tugs, tugs with all the might of its earthbound
body.

In moments it is followed by a second. They nuzzle and
play and scratch – fleas? I switch on the flashlight and for
one brief moment hold them in the red glare. Next
moment they have tumbled headlong down the hole.

Minutes pass. The boar? re-emerges. Nose beckoning, pushing towards the flashlight. He seems more disturbed by the glowing tree-trunk behind him. Disappears.

Five minutes. Ten? Then from somewhere away in the darkness comes the rhythmic sweeping of leaves. The badgers have emerged from a farther doorway, proclaimed it safe and are doing their housework. This time I catch only the red coals of their reflected eyes as their bodies dissolve into the gloom.

Wait in respectful silence, as after the last amen, then skirt the wood home through fields seeing small forms (stoats, weasels?) slinking through the fields, diving and surfacing like seals.

★　　★

One day, months later, I walked that way again and found the setts rammed with stout poles. Dry leaves scampered over the disused playground and collected in heaps inside the holes. No badger had played there or swept its doorway for a very long time.

3

June brought June rain hanging in strings from the sky.
They say, if trapped in a vessel, placed in the open, June
rain has magic properties.

This is a month of magic – of the goddess whose elder
flowers herald the summer solstice and the nuptials of corn
and wood gods. But for Round House – no illusions, a
stream of honest gum-boots and most of the June rain
water went to washing the mud from the floor.

There was Willi on his way to Quedgeley to select a
new parson (reversing the role of poet with patron of the
Living) head full of dismal theory about the family vault,
that when the Severn waters rise the bones of the
Haywards float.

Then there was the landlord saying 'I've been sent . . .'
for a change, 'to ask you to paint a picture for the village
to present Mrs Tucker who is leaving the store.' I pored
through reference sketches and roughs for a mystical
landscape which he stared at, then suddenly upped and
offed saying, 'Do a painting of the church.'

Strangely, as though he had ordered the weather, the rain strings suddenly snapped and in a flood of brilliant sunshine, new strings rose up from the ground – cleavers which sidled up stalks and walls that and vines writhed and climbed to the sky; while the Round House threatened to float away on a sea of grass, to be borne along on the reedy mass that erupted from under the stones.

Over the village walls, from garden to garden the news buzzed, in pub and store – the village hub humming wherever villagers could gather to pass the time of day against the noise of the highway, wherever they could salvage shreds of their once contained existence.

Hedges flowered – cool scented may, containing the highway smells, keeping the noise and fumes from the preserve of the lower village – in which quiet backwater, between river and lily pond, among chortling and shrieking wildfowl, in the still grey gaze of the church, I made some roughs.

Then it was hay time again – a time of whirling wheels.
Spiky wheels glimpsed in fields through hedges and
rubber wheels burning the lanes between hedges; great
wheels staggering under hayloads and small wheels
spinning down footpaths. Summertime brought a
profusion of wheels hurrying in all directions.

Suddenly, like exotic birds, there were gypsies at the
village corner, their red and yellow caravan a shock in the
singing green. A dark haired woman feeding a child, sat
propped on the swingle tree, while a man with sandy
whiskers sat whittling pegs in the grass.

He had bundles of ready-cut lengths, some ten inches
long and ringed at either end. In forty seconds with a few
deft strokes, he had halved the stick and made two pegs.
The pegs, then mounted astride a willowy strip called a
'spleeder' were sold for eightpence a dozen at fairs – the
gypsy's livelihood.

The grass was full of shavings. The man barely looked
up. Two horses dozed in the summer grass – an old brown
horse with a floppy under-lip and a young horse being
gently broken, trained to walk outside the shafts.

Against the restless flow of traffic I bought a dozen pegs
to be convinced in years to come that it was not all a dream.

4

Like the private music of a shell were the sounds of this
house in the hills. This house so far from the road; this
other shell without waterpipes to hiss and gurgle, or
switches to clack. Sounds were the wind, the birds, the
rain and fire, the murmurs of farming and forestry – a far
off passing aircraft, the postman's knock or hoof-fall on the
track, voices.

Voices wending along the rights of way – audible but
unintelligible; along the private carriage-way that turned
to the south, or along the eastern path to Norbury Camp.
This was the centre of silence, between the Iron Age camp
on the hill and the 'green-way' where the sheep walked,
the field where flint arrow heads were found, and the
Saxon mounds by the river. Layers of footfall or turning
wheel left ripples of tide on a millpond.

Voices of the families of farmworkers echoed among the
stones, imprinted voices, one of which might rise from
the past to say we were happy – were we happy?',
consider, and go away.

Between the ivy and the rose, the snowdrop and the
bluebell there were whispers. Layers of peace generated
peace and kind activities left kind spirits. Sometimes by
firelight against the timbre of the kettle, I would hear a
moan on the outer wall – lost spirit of the wind.

It was a constructive silence, a timeless spiritual webbing
that supported these windswept uplands. This land, cragged
and honed by keen-edged teeth of ice; these valleys locked
in frost and cotton-wool mist; secret as briar buds,
occluded; slyly cleft by the angled sun.

It conjured dreams that soared like hill-roads to
infinite, high horizons, dragging in turn, like hauled sails,
the folds of surrounding hills to converge in common
distance; or visions that plunged through leafy tunnels,
down to some intimate place in the depth of the mind's
recesses, charged as a flash on the retina.

Here, in reflection, memory coursed the antique ways of
human scale, filtering out poles, housing estates and even
the posturing pylons as it followed the haywaggon lanes –
teetering, tottering, loitering, dithering, frisking over
fields and rambling through forests, coiling and twisting
through convolutions of scenery: rushy meadows lined
with willows, geese, sheep and shining water, pale stone
cattle, mossy slates, pillars topped with lions or pommels,
vistas shrouded under ledges or tunnelled between high
yew hedges; an ever changing pageant drawn on the
ancient chart of stone; the stone that exuded from the
hills and re-formed in manor, farm and church, cottage
and village store; a pattern of rich rough walls strung out
in a lively collage.

Elsewhere one knew there were other places, downtrodden, angry or frantic. But here, bounded north and west by escarpments, south and east by the gradual incline to Thames and Evenlode, was preserved a pastoral Eden between hunks of high wild wold. Here intricate valleys were set like gems in a mount of indifferent paste; each brilliant in its own lustre, but with boring planes between, where the wolds, those passive lands, were prey to speedy high-roads, to air-strips and war-time structures. The Looking Glass world of each valley was complete within its frame, but merely to peer beyond, or to look over one's shoulder, was enough to shatter the glass, bringing one face to face with more sober reality.

139

One day beyond the Cotswold fringe, beyond the Thames and the Vale of the White Horse, I travelled a way that was signposted 'To the Village and the Downs'.

On, on it wound through tree-lined fields, past houses half-timbered and thatched, and horses filing to the gallop. Up, up it went to the top of the downs where it stopped by the ancient Ridgeway. From here I turned to look again at my eighteenth century landscape, but saw instead, from over the trees a vast industrial scene, the spread of Didcot Power Station, and Harwell Atomic Reactor, half shrouded in sunlit steam.

5

This summer of blue flowers and golden corn was turning into the 'best autumn for fifty years' with colour inching into the trees.

Beating had given up Ben, and now Ben, in turn, had given up the ROOSTER and gone instead to parts outside ROOSTERSHIRE to clear and plant for the Forestry Commission.

Connie's extension, the ever-boiling kettle, steamed away on the Fyreside heater, even when its mistress went to teach, which she did every Thursday at Cirencester Art School, doubling her sixteen mile there-'n-back journey by dumping her children in Cheltenham with Kath, the 'lesser crested' Hayward.

When the van coughed, spluttered and died, Connie traded the starter motor, the only salvageable piece, for another vintage van.

Now there were long mellow Indian-summer days, and with the start of the shooting season, guns crackling in woods most days of the week. There was Felicemas – the birthday of the second Messiah, and the Johns wafting through leaves with their feathery dogs. Walking to Needlehole I came across a party of nymphs in jeans, their flying hair plastered with autumn berries – Rebecca John and her cronies. Nearing the cottage heard cries for help from Mary and Phineas trying to lift a bed upstairs

through the manhole. Ran and was promptly attacked by
Edwina (dog) who put her teeth through my gum-boot.

One nippy night in October, the Harvest Festival supper
was held in the Manor hall, the only room of the old
mansion left since it was re-built. Everyone lined the long
tables. Logs blazed in the fireplace and the 'ladies
committee' bustled about with heaped plates under the
stern gaze of the squire's ancestors. The following day
there were elections and the temperature dropped still
further.

I searched for a thermometer, preferably antique, to
measure degrees of frost.

Unable to find one in any Chelt antique shop, I called on
Charlie and found him without his teeth.

'Thermometerth . . . uthed to have plenty of thothe' . . .
He rummaged in a huge black trunk for nearly ten minutes
while I perched apprehensively on the edge of a chair.

'Blatht . . .' he said at last, 'Don't know where they all
got to, but have a crithp' and he opened a bag of potato
crisps which had been buried forever at the bottom of the
trunk.

There was an elaborate, blue-leaved plant, rather like an
artichoke in his garden.

'Thath a thithle . . .' said Charlie.

Just before summer time ended (and clocks were put
back) Polly arrived.

Polly, a spotty bay mare belonging to Caroline John,
was allowed to stay in the top field, provided she didn't
eat sheep . . . the landlord's stipulation since one of his
uncle's horses had chewed the ears off prize sheep.

From horseback, the Cotswolds had a new perspective
. . . the extra elevation gave a view over hedge tops in a
way that walking or even driving never would. Now that
the 'best autumn for fifty years' plus a dash of frost, had
pinched the last ounce of colour into the leaves, hills and
valleys were afire . . . a soft fire, all bathed in misty light.

It was exhilarating riding over these hills . . . Polly
sweating and panting on her green feed, cavorting and
shying as the pheasants flew up. The air was full of
whiteness and lightness and the autumn dry stones pale and
shadowless.

143

I would, if I could, have stopped
time then in that climatic autumn
of the third year. The desire to view
the landscape from every crest, to
encompass every wood and embrace
the whole scope of colour and design.
I sought out the bridle-paths and
once rode to hounds, curious to learn
something of that love and its
traditional trails – trails I could not
otherwise have found for myself.
These were not the quiet
introspective ways of the
woodlanders, but something quite
different, brilliant and extroverted.
The early patterns that I had
experienced here, the simple
patterns of the landscape, the
horizontals through verticals, the
pegged down hills and the sun
juggling the shadows, had become
overlaid with reason . . . where crops
and fallow, where woods and pasture,
where walls were placed and why;
and why horsetails and goose-grass
grew here, and marjoram there.
From the central stillness the greater
plan had become laced with
movements of animals and men –
Now came a new pattern over the
whole . . . a pattern of authority
stamped out in drumming hooves by

the descendants of the makers of this
landscape – a pattern of the
privileged. For a while I was
initiated to a new ritual beat.

There seemed a sort of desperation about this beat. The
rhythm was urgent . . . unlike the rhythm of the
stonewallers whose evidence was oldest in this land . . .
unlike the rhythm of the hands that carved the mullions of
Cotswold windows and shaped the acres of woodland.

And over all there strode the pylons, whose grasping
shadows cast by steel fretwork, encased smaller checks
within the chequerboard of fields. The pylons . . . erect
but not proud, were strange in the habit of strangers who
are conquerors rather than friends.

6

Now it was winter. The landscape changed as storm
after storm, dark broom after broom, had swept away the
autumn softness, had whittled all to the barest bones, to
stones, green algae on trunks and limbs, to tumps and
hollows where leaves collected; clusters of rose hips along
the lanes and grey ghosts of traveller's joy looming in
hedgerows.

As Christmas lights went up in the town and commerce
hummed in the High Street, the auction market closed for
all time, and Charlie Fry, pushed by developers, sold out.

The sale began at ten thirty on a Thursday in Charlie's
front garden, the bidding proceeding urn by concrete urn,
stone by stone. Bundles of scrap had been thrown together,
old garden tools, the useless with the good, bundles of
brass rods, bundles of household things, dowry and
treasure chests spilling their contents, stained glass
windows, chimney pots and gnomes. A rustic lover and
his lass cast in concrete, lay in the grass. Someone stood on
them.

146

Charlie had new stuff, bought for the occasion, and guarded all week behind locked gates. Such lures as a grandfather clock, wound at last moment to show it would go – which it did, sixty seconds to the second backwards. Or a beautifully inlaid Victorian piano, obviously more ornamental than musical, which sure enough made the most horrible noise.

School desks, enough to fill a classroom, were impeccably arranged, while chairs were lined up for a setting of Les Chaises. The mirror department, propped against the firewood department, glinted at the apple boughs, while many a pub glass, engraved with flowers, filled the gap in the framing of some horific hall stand. Among the brass bedsteads, bed-pans and preserving jars, a grandaddy mangle was wearing a hat-box.

Everyone and his dog was there; all the rival dealers come for the pickings. One gent packed his van with bicycle spares, while another with a hand cart piled with washstands, blocked the traffic for half a mile down the Tewkesbury Road.

At the bottom of the yard, Charlie's own van and bandsaw were clearly labelled NOT FOR SALE.

There seemed to be more than a mere chapter ending with the closing of this funny place in the land of chimney pots and small brick houses; of knick-knacks, rabbits and rhubarb, and the little old man who made us laugh. Gypsies and gentry alike came here – and now a widened road was planned to replace the improbable stamping ground – to end a whole way of life. But this was progress.

Now snow fences were rising on high ground along the roads of this wintering land. St Paul's Epistle, round barrow, landmark whose larches lime-fresh that first spring had beckoned towards the endless woods, dells and intimate places, now frost-bitten brown, was tracing a smoke of marestails across the sky.

A kestrel gliding, just skimming the trees, drifting, drifting, black as a bat, bursting from the tops like a piece of flung bark, then sliding back from another angle, was eyed by robins in the snowberry hedge – two robins the colour of ripest peach who watched it with heads turned skywards, sideways, ready in a twinkling to dart for cover.

A squirrel surfaced from hibernation; a feather puppet on unseen strings, suspended, coursing the ground in quivers, remained in cover under the trees, while blackbirds, visible by their bills – two cigarettes that glowed in the dark, pecked and scratched in the depth of the thicket

But the sinister bird just drifted, drifted – a vampire hand playing sky scales.

High under the kestrel's eye, a storm fermented. Against a grill of yellowish cirrus was a brooding front from which shapes broke, dark, like air-ships, heading southwards, while a volley of white cannon smoke puffs detached themselves and hurtled east. The sky seemed divided against itself. Conifers stood like square-rigged masts.

To have stayed at this time would have given cause to reflect, to savour the woodsmoke, leaves, to see the next year's ground prepared, and to, like Minnie, dream by the fire and waken only to eat and dream, eat and dream like a cat.

1972

But I did not stay – and now, years later, recall on the hill where it started, the first flood of feeling, like new sap, rising over the stone walls, the sky flocks, the tumuli, the 'green ways' and gate in the cleft.

The gate stands ajar with its precincts depleted, the hilltop bare as a raided larder. Winds stir the seedheads and rattle the strands of dock. Of Woodhouse not a stone remains or bump in the grass.

Take wing with the gulls come ahead of the rising storm, planing by woods that are leafless and torn by new superstructures – a wasteland of pylons, a cat's cradle nest of wires cracking like locusts, rasping directions and stilling the birds.

Winds stir the seed-heads, moaning by hollow eves,
under the mossy tile, over the flaking door. Houses unlived
in fade, prey to mould, thorn and rat. Soon the distemper
flakes; soon rot invades the sill.

Winds caress silent walls, probing forgotten worlds,
scattering memories of once blooming flowers. A new
type of plant is replacing the cottage's eye bright and
meadow sweet, fostered flowers straight from the city hot
houses, conveyed with the townsmen by fast motorways.

Here hang the Needleholes, moths in a web. Boarded up
empty eyed, sunk in dry nettles.

Handspan does not fit old handspan; measure does not

meet with measure. Somewhere time has altered the
pattern. Footprint with footprint does not tally.

See where the ice has split the stone, the rain has rutted
the track, the rotting grass has mulched the bank and
formed a new ground level; the forest saplings have grown
to trees and within their strong, pale bars an ancient oak,
some centuries old, is grappling with fate.

Its lower trunk is cracked and wrinkled like a face that
has fought all weathers. Its limbs spreadeagled, thrust with
a force to bow the other trees, while one, unable to resist,
is strangled in a death-lock. Ugly and violent, yet
venerable are the rages of this tree.

If body strains to follow where the senses galloped before, where fingers traced the hillscapes through the leaves, finding some acres felled, some planted – change everywhere – and hearing from the hilltop the whining song of the road . . .

If peering through each open door brings only an empty sigh and a warning notice DUE TO BE MODERNISED . . .

Maybe at this moment, in the midst of reflection and change, one can turn back the stealing hands and see that here between sycamore and beech, there was once a clothesline strung, and the bright pegs danced in the frost – and there the bluebells and the parsley grew higher than the children's heads and the honey cats fossicked for fieldmice.

And here was the garden. Wipe the grime from the window pane and see it once again. Imagine, beyond the trees, the perspective leading away and away to those new twisty leaves first glimpsed beyond the glass.

Then as the senses stir and begin to mount and rise – running over the white grass, over and over the white grass, rough as a badger's pelt – they meet and mingle with the sun, seeking among the beech boughs the haunt of owl and nuthatch, clambering over the rootscape of mountains and small lakes, edging the wood sanicle and lighting the tapers of brome. And there you must leave to complete the tale, the wind, as it shakes the seed heads and whispers against the wall: 'The child of the imagination will forever run this way, barefoot over the badger grass to the sunlight in the trees – to where the spring pulse quickens.'

Round House

Once back within the silence, turn
To poise the sunlight on the stone,
To check the stippling code of leaves
To greet a self that lives alone.

Then slash the silence through with sound
As diamonds scribble words on glass;
The notes grid and corrode the air,
Light trembles on the threshold . . . Pass

The small but perfect selves of birds
Into the ever opening sky . . .
Then pace and pace the sounding floor,
And draw the curtains of the I.

William Hayward

Needlehole and
Little Needlehole

Alcot
Wood
House

Round House
well
Pinswell

Norbury
Camp

Hill
Barn

Tomtits
Bottom

Mill

1 MILE